ALETHIA SMITH

LOVE
FOR ALL
THE
WRONG
REASONS

Love for All the Wrong Reasons

Alethia C. Smith

Copyright

the information is without contract or any type of guarantee assurance.

The trademarks that are used are without any consent, and the publication of the trademark is without permission or backing by the trademark owner. All trademarks and brands within this book are for clarifying purposes only and are the owned by the owners themselves, not affiliated with this document.

ISBN No. 978-1-943409-32-7

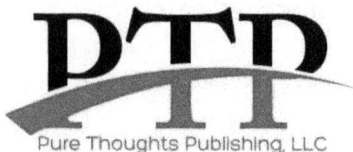

Pure Thoughts Publishing, LLC

www.purethoughtspublishing.com

Printed in the United States of America

Table of Contents

Copyright...3

Acknowledgements 7

Foreword 8

Introduction 11

Understanding You! 24

Standards...39

What Kept Me Going After Another Hit? 50

Forgiveness and the Healing Process: It's All about You

....66

One Template Is Not the Only Template.................82

The Single Life...91

Your Next Relationship 106

Sometimes People Do Change 116

Progress, Not Perfection 123

What I've Learned 128

About The Author 132

Acknowledgements

Without God, I would be nothing and without Him I would fail. It would be impossible for me to have a story to tell without Him so I must thank Him first. I must thank Him for being my everything in every stage of my life. I would also like to acknowledge my parents who have unconditionally loved me and encouraged me to reach my goals. I love you both more than I could ever explain. A special thank you also goes to my brother, his wife, and daughter. All three of you have impacted my life in an invaluable way and I love you all. To my friends, who are few in number but monumental in support, thank you for never leaving my side and always reminding me who I am. My final thanks goes to the man who gracefully, yet intensely, changed the plot of my story. Thank you for supporting me and telling me everything I needed to hear when I needed to hear it.

Foreword

"Sometimes People Do Change" is the title she chose for the portion of this book written about me: in everything described, explained and mentioned as it pertains to her experiences, I can see on her face and through her actions. As a man who had never received a "no" from a woman, things were quite different for me this time around. Now I know you're probably saying, "That's a lie," but allow me to explain. I've received many "no's" from many women but they were not sincere. My mother would tell me no when I'd ask for something as a child, only to get it for me later on when she felt like it. My sister would tell me I couldn't hang out with her and her friends, only to make a deal with me later in exchange for something. Therefore when I became eager and bold enough to talk to women, I was never prepared for a "no". I hadn't been trained on it, had no knowledge of what it really meant, nor had I truly experienced it.

Girls would say no to one question but then when rephrased, they'd respond with "maybe" or "I'll see". Those responses instilled the hope that maybe if I articulated my thoughts and words in a different way, a "yes" was sure to come. Sure enough, that's what continuously happened. Although I had become a master of articulation, stimulation and word manipulation, she was not falling for any of it. I spoke with the biggest words, the smoothest voice, shined the brightest smile (with the biggest gap) and still no progress. This told me that not only was she unimpressionable, but she had been hurt before. I chased her for years, but it wasn't until I gained a better understanding of this particular kind of woman, that I became aware of what I was doing wrong. You see, I chased and flirted, while all along I should have been pursuing. You may say what's the difference between pursuing and chasing; well I'm quite excited that you asked…

When chasing something, you may do it to recover what got away from you, stopping something or someone for a particular reason or simply because you forgot to include something. However, when in pursuit of something or someone, you do it wholeheartedly, withholding nothing because it's just that important and delicate. Nothing around you matters and no one near you can stop you. When I began to pursue, then and only then did I become knowledgeable of why I had failed so many times before. It was not time for her to be with me and I was not prepared to be with her as of yet. God planned it just right, so I'll just write that you've shown me how to love you the right way—the only way and for the right reasons.

Pseudonym: Fortune

Introduction

I was a teenager full of promise, excitement, and adventure, but then I met him. Suddenly my whole life became different. Maybe it wasn't suddenly, maybe I just wasn't paying attention. Everything changed. My focus was on how good he made me feel and how important I thought I was when I was with him. I found myself saying, "I love you" at an early age, not knowing everything that simple, yet heavy phrase, would entail. But boy would I find out. At first, my definition of love was simple; accept someone for who they are and be there for them. But in a way I am thankful to him because I found out that love is so much more.

I had known of him since I was in elementary school, but we officially met online (Facebook). I gave him my number and he called me the same night. Our first conversation was one to remember. It made me feel special and made me smile when I thought about it. When I finally said yes to be his girlfriend, everything felt perfect. He made me laugh and taught me not to take things so seriously all the time. He had a way with words, and since I had never really had a serious relationship, nothing was out of place for me. As a teenager, I thought our relationship couldn't get any better. He respected me and accepted me and that's all I thought I needed. I could talk to him about anything; things were just that good. We were even talking about marriage. Yeah, I know, young right? But what I didn't know is what would happen as we stayed together. These are the things I was not prepared for.

We went through a lot as a young couple. There were many breakups and as a matter of fact, there were too many for me to remember them all. But I can still remember the first one. Not long after we broke up, he posted a picture on Facebook with another young lady who was his new girlfriend. Sign number one that I ignored because I was so in love. He had already moved on and I was still standing there looking stupid. When he came back, I took him back. Well, little did I know, this would not be the last time. It happened, again and again, and again, and well you get the picture. Each time we broke up, he found a new girlfriend in less than a month. The sad part wasn't that he totally disregarded me; it was that *I* disregarded *myself*. He showed me who he really was by repeatedly attempting to develop relationships with other females and I showed how weak I was by letting him back in my life every time. It wasn't one of those situations where I was approached with deceit; I saw things with my own eyes! I hadn't placed enough value on myself because if I had, this would have been

LOVE FOR ALL THE WRONG REASONS

over long before I started to feel all of those negative emotions. Because he got into relationships so fast, I had no doubt he was cheating. Trust dwindled and I became Inspector Gadget. Every chance I got, I went through his phone or his social media accounts. I found something every time. You can add this to my list of mistakes, too. With the knowledge of his disloyalty, that should have been enough for me to leave, but I stayed.

For the first year of our relationship, he couldn't visit my home because my parents were not allowing me to have male company yet. He waited until he could and I thought that was the sweetest thing. What puzzles me now is why didn't I think that he was *supposed* to wait? Why didn't I think that he was *supposed* to think that much of me? I'm worth every of second of the wait, right? That wasn't the only thing he waited for either. I was a virgin when we met and I had every intention to stay that way until we were married. He told me he was a virgin too; I think that's also the first lie he told me (I don't know why I was so naïve to believe that one). He thought that's what I wanted to hear so that's what he said. Sign number two that I ignored because I was so in love. I gave up the cookie, y'all. You can judge me, I know I'm not the only one who has had this experience, but I will regret that for the rest of my single life. It was not what I imagined. It's even more unpleasant now that I have to remember that it was something so precious that he seemed not to care about. It's something that I definitely cannot get back. I thought after three years he was worthy of the cookie, and I thought he would stay. Lesson learned: NO MAN IS WORTHY UNTIL HE IS YOUR HUSBAND!

Here I am thinking that this is going to be my husband and we're going to be together forever, but does anybody notice an important piece missing here? Yeah, God was missing. Your relationship with God is more important than your relationship with any man or woman. I thought giving my all, both sexually and emotionally, would make him stay, but you can't make anyone stay anywhere they don't want to be, no matter how good you are to them. I *still* don't understand why giving someone *everything* wouldn't make them want to stay, but that's the reality of it. So that was one of many mistakes: I neglected God. And for that, I am truly sorry and I don't ever want to do that again. I "consulted" God and got the answers I *wanted* to get from Him and continued to do what I *wanted* His will to be. I hadn't taken the time to establish the relationship with God that I had established with this guy. My mind was all over the place...all over the wrong places. I was confused about so much and I lost sight of what I really wanted for myself because I felt pressured, especially from him, to get married straight out of high school. I had convinced myself that it was the right thing to do so we would avoid more fornication, but if anyone asked me to give them another reason for doing it, I probably couldn't give a legitimate one.

When we got engaged, I was in college and that is when it set in that he was going to be my husband and I thought all would be well. Not long before this, he had gotten in a car accident and sustained a serious injury. During that time we were broken up and once again, he had already started something new with someone else. However, I was so much in love that I still felt obligated to check on him. I was at school in Wingate, North Carolina and he had to be rushed to the hospital in Charlotte, North Carolina. At the time I did not have a car, so I called a friend and asked her to take me to the hospital to see someone who no longer belonged to me. It was awkward to sit in the waiting room with people who had no obligation to have any connection or relationship with me, but it was something I felt like I had to do.

I can still remember this day so vividly. When I was finally able to see him, all I really wanted to do was cry. To see someone I loved so much hurt—hurt me just as much. I didn't know what to say; I just wanted to take all pain and memory of this horrible accident away for him, but I couldn't. So after a few minutes, I kissed his forehead and told him to get better. I walked out of that hospital room not expecting to see or talk to him again, but he came back. Yes, I wanted him to come back, but I wasn't sure that he would this time. He came back and *proposed*. It was the sweetest thing he ever did for me. We were at a bowling alley and twelve random people came up to me giving me single red roses at random moments. "All of Me" by John Legend was playing and when I turned around from a bowl, he was on one knee…his hurt knee. Of course I said yes. I thought this was the man for me and I was the only woman for him. Saying yes only set me up for greater hurt and heartache when things went haywire though. He put a ring on my finger…but I took it off. Marrying him would have taken my life in a totally different direction, one that I would probably be unhappy with.

The issue was that my parents did not agree with it. I hadn't finished college yet and that was the main reason they preferred that I wait. We were thinking, however, it's just an engagement; we're not getting married tomorrow (or ever), but sometimes your family and friends can see the end of a relationship while you're still at the beginning. My dad said he would discuss his issue with him, but, I didn't believe it was done in full detail and honesty. After all that time, I thought my fiancé would be more than happy to talk to him and we would get our relationship back on track. However, right after we broke up, he was starting a "new beginning for an everlasting love" with someone else. So for him, our relationship must've been over long before we finally *said* it was. He had been posting pictures and declaring love for someone else already. There was no regard for my feelings or the love that I thought we shared. Everyone that I thought supported *us* was now supporting him and his new girlfriend (she wasn't really new, he had left me and gone to her before, too). Another lesson: don't get the loyalty your mate's family shows confused with loyalty for you. When it's all said and done, his family will be in his corner. I learned this lesson more than once; his family and friends don't have to maintain a relationship with you once the tie is cut. Of course, they will cheer you on when things are good, but their loyalty is to him, not you.

I had no doubt he knew what love was; he just had a messed up way of showing it sometimes, which changed my own perception of it. I began to accept and adapt to the kind of love he showed and I was convinced

---

LOVE FOR ALL THE WRONG REASONS

that it was the love I needed. It became my normal even though I knew there was a better way; I just chose to settle for what I got since I had been with him for so long. Those who were used to him pacified him, and I was no different because I allowed him to get away with a lot. We often treat men like adolescents, pacifying them, and helping them justify their actions. This same pacification develops a pattern and until he is treated in a different way, he will always attract, and be attracted to, a woman that caters to what he's used to. He knew that as long as he played on the fact that my love was unconditional, he would always have me. He knew that my confidence and respect for myself couldn't have been where it should've been if I continued to take him back after every breakup. He had lost respect for me and I must have lost respect for myself along the way as well. I must admit, he was pretty smart about that and I was weak. I had no clue what kind of power I had in my femininity alone. Ladies, we have to remember that we are the prize! When I came to this realization, I knew I could no longer focus on his needs and wants and remain oblivious to the blessing I was to him. This had to be my attitude from that moment on; I was no longer going to be his pacifier.

I was not wrong to love him. To love is never wrong, and you should always love right and love strong.

LOVE FOR ALL THE WRONG REASONS

My reasons, however, were not sufficient. I loved him for who I wanted him to be. I loved him for whom he made me feel like. I loved him for tolerating me because I now realize that it couldn't have been love that he felt for me. I *should* have loved him for who he really was and not who he *said* he was. I was under the impression that I had a man who was willing to go through valley lows and mountain highs with me, but that's what I wanted, not what I really got. I loved the *idea* of someone loving me back. For me, all of those were the wrong reasons to love. After all of this, he married someone else three weeks after our last breakup. One could look at the situation many different ways: maybe he fell in love just that quickly, or he had been involved with her the whole time. Did it hurt? Of course it did. Certain words would trigger anger and I was on the verge of hate. Movies, pictures, memories…I wanted all of it to go away. The very things that I adored while I was with him became the very things I disdained when we went our separate ways. I even thought maybe if I had a really bad accident and got amnesia from it, I'd be better. Would I show my hurt? Yes, but only to those who would accept me and love me regardless. I was upset with myself for allowing it to hurt, for allowing myself to fall so deeply in love and be so weak for someone who didn't feel the same way. At that point I wanted to be selfish too. I wanted to worry about my feelings and no one else's. I wanted to break hearts and move on like nothing ever happened. The problem with that is that's not who I am and I just couldn't do that to anyone.

Even with all the unnecessary pain he put me through, I just couldn't bring myself to cause him or anyone else any hurt. Sure I thought about riding to his house just to slash tires or break a few windows, but that wouldn't have solved anything; it would just have given me a court date. I didn't deserve to be hurt this way, but that didn't give me the right to torture anyone else. I believe payback should come in a different way-in a way that would have made me happy and would have hurt him without laying a hand on him. Eventually he would have gotten what he deserved and it wouldn't have resulted in me going to jail. In determining what would make me happy, I came to the conclusion that loving <u>me</u> more than I have ever loved anyone was the best way to do it. I had to reestablish myself and start fresh. I had to evaluate myself and get to know the new me because the love I had for him changed who I was. It changed me into someone I had never met before, but I started liking her. She's stronger than the old me, and she has a little more experience. Even though her heart had been torn, broken,

LOVE FOR ALL THE WRONG REASONS

and stomped on, she still wanted love and she still wanted to give love. She still had more to give even when she thought someone else took it all. That's the amazing thing about her; she still has more.

I couldn't tell you how this thirst and hunger for love evolved. I couldn't tell you how in the name of all that is human nature I could still be open to love and relationships, but I am. I can't allow the mistakes of one man to define my whole love life or stop me from finding my real true love. I am going to give the *right* man the permission to love me the way I deserve; but I have to heal first. There's nothing wrong with flirting and a little conversation. There was no rush, although I believed it would help me if I showed my ex just what he was missing by seeing me with someone else. Healing is a process and I had to complete that process. That is one reason for this book. Airing it all out took me through every emotion. I remember good times and bad; I see my mistakes and his, and I remember what I've learned. These are lessons I will take with me through the rest of my life and share with everyone I can.

Through all of my pain and brokenness, I can see the light at the end of the tunnel. My story, my pain will be lessons not only for me, but for every young lady (and young man) that I have an impact on or come in contact with. My scars will heal, my mind will be at ease, and my heart will rejoice in the hope of new, true, unquestionable love! The best thing about an ending is the hope for a new beginning. Getting over someone with whom you've had so many firsts is not easy, but it will get easier. It got easier as I wrote this book, and it got even easier when I realized what I had ignored for so long and acknowledged what I really deserved. This is my truth, and I am not ashamed of it.

During the healing process, I had to come to a point of not feeling sick when I thought about him or what he had done to me. Although I was initially disappointed in myself for allowing all of this to happen, I can see now that I had to learn these lessons to become who I am today. I had to have this heartbreak to appreciate the process of being put back together again. I had to enjoy watching myself bloom after a long, cold season of my life, and I am proud of what I see when I look in the mirror. I don't feel sorry for myself, but I do feel sorry for him. That sounds strange but let me help you understand. I sacrificed more than I thought I ever would for him. I loaned money, gave my body, opened my heart, rearranged plans, went against the wishes of my parents, suffered through changes in friendships, all in hopes of becoming his wife. Those are just a few. So think of all the things I would have continued to sacrifice if we had married. So every bit of love, sacrifice, pleasure, and fulfillment that I tried to give to him will now go to someone else who will appreciate it and never let it go. So yes, I feel sorry for him and what he will never have again. I feel sorry for him because there's so much more growing that he has to do and he doesn't even realize it. You'd be surprised to know how many people came to me, or someone I'm connected to, and said they were happy for me because our relationship was over. Even some of his family members agreed because they thought he was no good for me.

I've said all this to help someone avoid the same mistakes. When you are looking for a relationship, make sure that you know who you are first. Don't allow someone else's companionship define who you are or who you want to be. Don't depend on anyone to show you love before you show it to yourself. Let people in to get to know the real you. Let love happen, and let things take their course. Throughout this book, I will give insight on how I chose healing and happiness over hurt and anger. It takes a willing and open mind to understand each process and patience to get through it. By the end, I hope that you will be inspired and redefine your reasons for love.

LOVE FOR ALL THE WRONG REASONS

Understanding You!

You know your favorite color, your favorite foods, and your favorite shopping places. Have you ever thought about the smallest things that make you upset? Have you ever paid attention to the smallest things that make you smile? What about the things that make you nervous and the little things you do to cope with your nerves? Before you can allow anyone in, you have to be able to predict your own actions. Your strengths and your weaknesses can alter who you are when you are paired with someone else. For instance, when I was with this particular guy, I had no clue how much patience I had. As a matter of fact, I initially thought I was very impatient and I refused to let anyone toy with my emotions and allow them to walk over me. However, in that very characteristic that I thought was my strength, I also found my weakness. Patience is truly a virtue, but it is not a substitute for poor judgment. Allowing the same thing to happen over and over again and expecting different results is simply poor judgment.

'Tis true that in all things you should be patient because you do not know what you have been protected from. Patience, though, does not mean to wait on someone to realize just *who* you really are! My mistake was waiting. I waited for him to see how loyal I was and

LOVE FOR ALL THE WRONG REASONS

how good of a woman he had. All the while, I had ignored the fact that he clearly didn't see this from the beginning. You can't continue to wait for someone to see your worth when there are people who will see it immediately. Every time we broke up, I would let him back in because I thought he had learned his lesson. Since he had gotten a taste of what it felt like to be with someone else, he knew he had the best already, right? Wrong. This, in turn, caused my trust for him to diminish even more.

After going back and forth about marriage or whether he thought I was the one for him, and constantly breaking up, I had no inclination to trust him. With no trust, it was hard for our already weak relationship to last. I don't believe either of us was really ready for marriage, and it took a long time for me to accept that. We loved each other and we wanted to stay together, but it obviously wasn't meant to be. For a while, things would be good and we'd be on cloud nine, but when things didn't go the way either of us thought they should, we were broken up again and he was with someone else. Know your strengths, but don't allow them to cripple you like I did. My patience blinded me. I kept being the "good woman", and I kept waiting for him to come back.

LOVE FOR ALL THE WRONG REASONS

My loyalty was proving what kind of woman I was, but I had lost confidence in the process.

I had put myself in a box; I know I have my flaws just like everyone else, but somehow he convinced me that no one else was willing to deal with mine. When he had to wait a year to visit me at my parents' house, I was constantly reminded that no one else would have done that; no one else would have waited that long to see his girlfriend on a regular basis. I would ask a lot of questions such as, "Do you love me?" "How do you feel about me?" or "What is your favorite thing about me?" He would answer them, but not without complaining about the questions. I began to think something was wrong with that, too. Why did I have to ask all these questions? Did I need validation? Then it dawned on me that if I had to ask, maybe he wasn't showing it enough. I am the type of person that likes to *feel* what you feel about me. If you tell me how you feel, that's beautiful, but I need to know it even without hearing a word. I need to know that I'm one of the most important people in your life every day. Now I know and understand that that's *not* too much to ask for.

Throughout the process, he also made me feel like honoring the wishes of my parents was not something I was obligated to do. They did not want us to get married

LOVE FOR ALL THE WRONG REASONS

so soon, and after constantly hearing what he and his parents had to say, I was determined to live my life for me...or was it for someone else? I had become so lost in everyone else's desires that it was hard for me to determine what *I alone* wanted. I was smothered with questions of "what if" and "how will you..." It made me want to run away from everyone. When making such heavy decisions, we have to remember who actually has to live with the decision. I should not have allowed so many opinions to penetrate my way of thinking.

I now know that even when I do not necessarily agree with my parents, it is still perfectly okay to consider what their opinion is and weigh my options. So if a man can't handle me honoring my parents, we can't have a relationship. There is no way I can expect him to honor me if he encourages me to dishonor someone else. Certain people's opinions matter greatly to me, whether I agree with them or not. My parents gave me life and took care of me when I couldn't take care of myself. It would be disrespectful to them, in my opinion, if I had chosen to completely disregard how they felt. Everyone doesn't agree with that, but I am perfectly okay with these characteristics about myself and anyone who can't handle them doesn't deserve me.

LOVE FOR ALL THE WRONG REASONS

Before I met him, like every other girl, I had my life mapped out in my head and getting married so young was not a part of the plan. As a matter of fact, getting married was not even a part of the plan. However, I wanted to change that for him. If getting married was the stipulation, I was going to follow through with it. It was for all the wrong reasons; I kept punishing myself with the thought that I would not find anyone else who would be willing to love me after so long. I was certain that no one else could tolerate my moods, listen to me overreact about little things, or try to understand me the way he did.

For a long time, I clearly struggled with insecurities and lack of confidence. Finally it dawned on me that those characteristics could easily be seen through my interactions with people. This had to change immediately. I started to evaluate myself on a daily basis, and I became more familiar with my imperfections. I had to consider everything from my appearance to the amount of patience I had and even the way I handled my money. It was an eye-opening, rewarding experience. In this evaluation, I also found myself better communed with God. My entire posture changed. I became more concerned with my prayer life and how I could make myself better.

LOVE FOR ALL THE WRONG REASONS

In developing a better relationship with God, I started using different ways to communicate and spend time with Him. I started writing my prayers in a prayer book. This amazingly showed me my spiritual growth. My prayers were not always about saving the hearts of my family and friends, but now they are. I didn't always pray for patience or the willingness to forgive those who have hurt me, but I do now. Thank you God for growth. I also started putting more of my heart into worshipping Him. Even though I feel like the biggest crybaby ever, I feel so much more in touch with God, and whatever is weighing me down seems so insignificant. It was closer to God that I extended my definition of love and the right reasons to love someone that I am developing a relationship with. My reasons to love may not be the same as yours; my reasons are not the Holy Grail. My right could be your wrong. I had fallen in love because I thought he possessed the qualities that I needed and he became the reason I felt good about myself. I thought, "Wow, I got his attention?" A decision had to be made here; I had to change the way I viewed myself and it couldn't be contingent upon a man's feelings towards me.Because of this, I took back my power. I would no longer delegitimize my pain for his comfort or to avoid shame. This was one of the major components of how I

LOVE FOR ALL THE WRONG REASONS

got through all of this; I definitely could not have done it without God. During the phase of insecurity and lack of confidence, I continued to foster pointless and unhealthy relationships, carry deadweight, and entertain negative vibes. I continued to communicate with people that meant me no good and had no intentions of encouraging me to reach my fullest potential. I allowed people to use me because I thought it was their way of showing me that they needed me. I had to open my eyes to the fact that there is a huge difference between being loyal to someone and being available for them to use you when necessary.

Along with understanding your strengths and weaknesses, I also believe that being able to control your emotions and your reactions to any circumstance is profoundly important. I understand that certain situations can make us angry, but they should not turn us into totally different people. When something or someone has made you angry, you should learn to evaluate the situation and yourself to see where even *you* may have been wrong. This allows you to make better judgments and avoid making the same mistakes later on. Just because you're angry does not give you an excuse to take it out on someone else. I guess what I'm trying to describe to you is temperament, ladies and gentlemen.

LOVE FOR ALL THE WRONG REASONS

I'm not telling you to hide your feelings, by all means please don't do that! I'm saying to express them in a way that doesn't cause even more anger for yourself or anyone else. Sure, you want that person to hurt, that's understandable. You want them to taste their own medicine, but after that, what happens? Find a different outlet that will allow you to freely express yourself and actually solve the problem. Where do you think the idea for this book came from?

I personally believe that there are different ways to love and everyone loves differently. I love hard and unconditionally. Even though that man put me through a whole lot of unnecessary things, I love him. I'm not afraid to tell anyone that, but I love him in a different way now. See, before I was *in love*, making sacrifices, admiring him, adoring his appearance, accepting his blemishes, and all that good stuff. Now, I love him the way I should love someone I once knew: a distant, teachable memory. I realize that things can never be the same; there has been too much pain, too much *unnecessary* pain. So I just have love *for* him. My point is, you should know *how* you love so that you can prepare your mate and yourself. Based on that, they can tell you whether or not they can handle your love, saving you some embarrassment. If it is hard for you to forgive

LOVE FOR ALL THE WRONG REASONS

someone, easy for you to fall in love, or if giving up on someone is hard for you to do, then you and your mate should discuss all of this. Be sure of what you can deal with. Are you okay with a man that has stinky feet? Can you compromise with a man who has a very busy schedule? If a man has no knowledge whatsoever about cars, can you deal with going to the mechanic for every single thing that is wrong with your car? The list could go on. Don't be afraid to say you need all the "nutritional facts" before you decide to consume something. Get to know your love and your mate's love so you know how it will affect you in the near and far future and know these things so they're not abused. My ex knew that no matter what, I would still love him and in a way, this was my downfall. My love was so strong and intoxicating that I just wouldn't let go, and he took advantage of it each time he decided to leave and come back. If your mate gives off the vibe that they're not ready for what you're ready for, then do not waste your time thinking that it is your divine assignment to change their mind.

To be able to love someone, you have to know the qualities that attract you. So what attracts you? What are some things that you do not want in a companion? Do you want the standard tall, dark, and handsome? Are you more concerned with inner qualities than physical

LOVE FOR ALL THE WRONG REASONS

appearance? What are you willing to compromise on? After you have found out who you are, you can readily tell someone else what you need. Past experiences can also take you through the process of elimination–trust me, I know. Once again, I'll use myself as an example. My past relationships have shown me exactly what I don't want. I don't want a man that has to be pushed to make himself better; he needs ambition. I'm not his mother so I don't want to have to remind him of his responsibilities. I want a man that had motivation *before* I met him. As a matter of fact, combining our motivation should inspire others to go after their dreams and achieve much more! I don't want a man that settles for just anything or whatever comes the fastest or easiest. The term, "best" was created to make a distinction between what is good and what is better than good; so there is no reason to be okay with mediocrity when you are more than capable of exceeding the minimum. I want a man that will agree to volunteer in a soup kitchen with me because he understands my love for helping people and the value of serving others.

There is nothing more attractive than a man that is eager for an education and a constantly improving life, one that is not okay with settling because he wants so much more. I don't want a man that allows others to influence his final decisions. At some point we all need advice, but that advice should not dictate every single choice we make. My man should have his own mind and be persuaded only by the will of God and what will be best for him and his family (and our relationship, when it's serious). I want a man that still thinks I'm beautiful with my hair tied up and sweatpants on. A man that takes pride in providing for his own and loving me unconditionally is what I want. I think you get the picture now. I had to get to know myself so that I would know what I want and need in a relationship. Just know what will *complement* or enhance your fly, not just match it. Get to know yourself; that's a beautiful process.

Knowing yourself means loving yourself. Learn to accept what others may view as flaws or deal-breakers. Modify what *you* want to and make sure it's for the benefit of you! You'd be amazed at how easy it will be for the right man to love the real, unfiltered you. While you wait on Mr. Right, make sure you are experiencing life. Take up new hobbies, take trips with your friends or your family members, make investments in yourself and properties, volunteer in your community, and make sure you are happy. Being single should be all about you; the focus shouldn't be on when the next man will enter your life. Focusing on what's next will only make you

LOVE FOR ALL THE WRONG REASONS

unmindful of what is going on now. Therefore, if you haven't reevaluated yourself in the meantime, when a good guy comes along, he could very well receive an incomplete, unhealed version of you, which only yields the same unwanted results. While I'm single, I am choosing to treat myself and love myself more every day. I've taken short notice, small getaways, bonded with more people, experimented with new hairstyles, changed my wardrobe, and found out so much about myself throughout this process. It makes you appreciate yourself and show you what you can offer someone else.

Another vital part of understanding you is being able to understand your faith. Being unequally yoked to God will only cause problems in your relationship, unless it is not a major factor in your life. You and your mate should not have to argue about whether to use the Qur'an or the Bible. People from different religious backgrounds make things work all the time, however, I think your beliefs should be coherent in a way that, if you have children, there won't be any confusion on where or how the family will worship. Faith is also a factor in determining whether or not you and your mate will have a sexual relationship or not. Some people believe you should test the waters before you get married to see if you're compatible, whether that is through premarital sex or premarital cohabitation. Others simply believe that fornication is a sin and should be treated that way and living together only leads to temptation. Your faith can also affect the way you choose to discipline your children in the future. While some believe that spanking their children should be a part of the disciplinary plan and is clearly stated in the Bible, others believe that kind of punishment is too harsh. Find the common ground.

A firm belief in a higher power (God for me) can bring a relationship through the toughest of times. He can heal any wounds and change any heart. Any and everything can be solved through him. God can be the outlet that the both of you need when there is a problem. You can confide in friends or family, but it's always better to take it to God. If you tell family about your problems or anything that your mate has done wrong, they will hold it against him even when you have forgiven him. Allow God to guide the both of you in your love and relationship and you can never go wrong. Listen to Him and don't try to change His will because His way is always better than yours. Stop hearing what you *want* to hear, and open your ears to what God is really telling you.

Throughout the course of our relationship, we went to church, we even prayed a few times together.

LOVE FOR ALL THE WRONG REASONS

Being submissive in your marriage and to your husband was a highly emphasized in the church where his family worships. I had read the scripture before so I knew what it meant. However, being submissive is not synonymous with not using or having your own mind. It means that you are married to someone who has a relationship with God and he is capable of leading you in a way that pleases God. It does not mean, "Do what I say because I'm the man." Nor should it evoke a certain fear in you that is shown all over your face when he talks to you. I watched a few of the women there and their interactions with their husbands and it made me skeptical. It was as if they said the "wrong thing", embarrassed their husbands, or showed an otherwise non-submissive demeanor, they'd put a stain on their relationship or ruin its perfect presentation to others. I did not want to become one of those women.

Our faith was coherent and we knew how our household would operate concerning religious matters. This was another reason I stayed. I am a Sabbath keeper and I observe the biblical feasts that are closely aligned with the Jewish tradition and so did he. For a lot of people that seems strange and usually no one wants to give up their Saturdays or their regular routine to come to church. When celebrating and participating in the feast days, a Sabbath could be on any day of the week. Therefore, any man who pursues a serious relationship with me would have to understand that and since a lot of them don't, once again, I had limited myself to being with him. What I didn't think about was the fact that if *God* sends me a man, these things should be the least of my worries. Seeking God would lead the right man in my direction, equipped with everything I need and everything I could ever want. So did I really understand my faith in God? Did I really trust Him to supply my *every* need? No. I chose to stay in toxicity without considering how much better God's plan is if I would just tap into my faith.

LOVE FOR ALL THE WRONG REASONS

Standards

My dad always told me not to set my standards so high that the pope or Jesus couldn't meet them. I always thought it was comical, but it's the truth. Ladies, we have to remember that no man is perfect, but his imperfections do not justify stupidity, either. He may not always get it right, but after finding out what you want and need, he should get it right more times than not. There are just some things that are a part of chivalry and there is no reason for it to be compromised. You are a queen and you should be treated as one every day, not just Valentine's Day or your birthday. He should open doors for you, bring you flowers just because, and notice new outfits or new hairstyles because the simple things matter. It should not be a problem for him to do small things that matter greatly to you. If you want a man that will buy you whatever you want, there is nothing wrong with that, but he should not feel used or as if he's in a relationship with a "gold-digger".

It is not unreasonable to want a man with a career, morals, and respect; you just can't expect the man not to make mistakes. However, when a man has made a pattern of making the same "mistakes", they become *choices*; this means you have a choice to make as well. We can't allow a man to step out on us multiple times and continue saying, "He just made a mistake. I forgave him and he won't do it again" when you know full well that he will. Every time you take him back, he takes some of your strength and each time he becomes less and less serious about you. He figures that he can do anything and you'll always accept his apology and reconcile with him. Whether you admit it or not, each time you lose trust as well. I know because I did it; I had a revolving door with his name on it. I'd let him back in with the knowledge that if something went wrong, we would just repeat the cycle.

You have to be firm. Set a standard for your suitors to meet and stick to it. For instance, being faithful should not be a fading phenomenon or surprising commodity. Once the two of you have made a commitment to date exclusively, loyalty and faithfulness should come in the package. It should not come as a surprise when you see that your man chooses to create a firm bulwark for any female that tests his obligation to you. Think of all the men you've admired and use them to set your own standard. The real point is making sure the man fulfills your needs and desires. Your desires shouldn't be unreasonable and you should be willing to understand and compromise on some things. Sure, a man

LOVE FOR ALL THE WRONG REASONS

will be a man, but your man shouldn't be just *any* man. You should feel free around him, willing to be open and be yourself. Being with him should only bring you joy, excitement, and anticipation for the next time you will be with him.

There is nothing wrong with a man making you feel good about yourself. The problem, however, is when you allow that man to be the *only reason* you feel good about yourself. No amount of love from anyone should surpass the amount of love you already have for yourself. I should have remembered how special and irreplaceable I was *before* he made me feel that way. I became extremely dependent on him and I needed his endorsement for everything. I wanted him to approve of my body, the music I listened to, and even the clothes I wore. It was no longer a matter of how content I was with who I was. Although our moments were special, I should not have allowed them to define us or to define me. What should have defined us was our foundation and unbreakable bond, but we know now that that bond was pretty breakable. How do I know that it couldn't have been love? Love shouldn't make me feel worthless even if things don't work out. Love shouldn't make me question what is wrong with me, and it shouldn't make me feel sick to my stomach when I think about

LOVE FOR ALL THE WRONG REASONS

everything that I dealt with to try to make this relationship work.

Love is a constant teacher and nurturer. We experience it in several different forms, whether it's through a friendship, a relationship, or from God and family. Each form varies and teaches us new lessons, subtly altering our perspectives and changing the course of our lives. So what *should* love feel like? Each person should have their own definition, but in some way, they will all have similarities. For me, love should feel godly. It should be unquestionable, unconditional, to be completely honest about it, I shouldn't even be able to describe it. I should smile every time I think about it. Pictures or words can't do it any justice, but you will know when you see it. Again, the answer is different for everyone, but each answer points to a common denominator: happiness. When you think about the love you have for, or with someone, you want to be able to associate happiness with it; it's only right. In relationships, however, love doesn't always come easy. What I mean is, the *feeling* may come easy, but the *act* sometimes doesn't. We all yearn for someone to love us the way we want to be loved, nothing more, and nothing less.

LOVE FOR ALL THE WRONG REASONS

Your companion will not always get it right the first time, which is why it is perfectly acceptable to teach him or her how to love you. Guide him on how to interpret your emotions, let him know how you like to show affection, and be upfront with what you refuse to compromise on. Teaching him how to love you shouldn't turn into you being his mother, though. Some things are obvious such as, the way he speaks to you, how he touches you, and how he cares for you. You should not have to explain that yelling at you makes you nervous because he shouldn't yell at you in the first place. The way he touches you shouldn't make you fear for your life; it should make you feel alive. How he cares for you should be the closest thing you can compare to the care that God has for you. The same applies for women; a man should have confidence that his woman is not going to add to the weight that is already on his shoulders. A relationship should not be a burden for either of you. You should create a space for each other that brings peace and eliminates stress or pressure.

There should be no doubt in your mind that your significant other will treat you with the upmost respect and always accept you for who you are. At no point is it okay for you to feel belittled, betrayed, or forgotten and if you ever do, it should not go unnoticed. When you let it

LOVE FOR ALL THE WRONG REASONS

slide the first time, what grounds do you have to stand on if you try to make a big deal out of it the next time he does it? A man does what he is *allowed* to do, and when he is given room for error, he will experiment to see how much you will tolerate. Once more, let me be your example. There were multiple occasions where I caught him having inappropriate or suspicious conversations. After I "addressed" it, we moved on; I never handed out real consequences for his actions. Although this did not give him the right to do it, it gave him the freedom. Establish your standards and know your limits; it will save you a lot of time and help you avoid heartache.

There is no greater love than the love that God has for me; He sent his only son to die for me. The thing about this love is He has never given up on me even when I turned away from Him. He was always there just waiting for me to realize how much I am worth! There should be no room for doubt or worry, and that's how I should feel when I think about love. I don't have to question whether He will be with me tomorrow because He will. I don't have to wonder if He will give up on me because His Word says He will never forsake me. I don't need to be someone else to make Him love me because He loves me just as I am: rough around the edges, goofy, difficult, faults and all. If no one else is there, God is.

LOVE FOR ALL THE WRONG REASONS

Along with his unconditional love, God gave us examples in his word to show us what love looks like.

Couples like Hannah and Elkanah and Ruth and Boaz are beautiful, biblical examples when you think about love and standards. Hannah was one of Elkanah's two wives. Unfortunately, Hannah could not give birth to any children and this hurt her deeply because his other wife did not have this issue. In those times, it was a sign of social status to be able to give birth to children, and of course, it would help carry on the family name. Even though she was infertile, when it was time for Elkanah to give portions to his wives and children, he did not forget about Hannah. As a matter of fact, he gave her a "worthy portion" (1 Samuel 1 KJV). Elkanah thought Hannah deserved to be treated no differently predicated on what she could or could not give him. He knew she was special.

Elkanah truly loved Hannah, and he did not make a big deal about her not being able to have children. He didn't even understand why it made her weep so much; he thought she would be happy just to be with him, and it hurt him to see that she wasn't. The point that I want to emphasize here is the fact that Elkanah did not constantly remind her of her infertility. Instead, he loved her beyond what one could argue to be a flaw. His love was

---

LOVE FOR ALL THE WRONG REASONS

not based on what she could give him or do for him, he loved her *unconditionally*. Not only that, God loved her, too. Hannah's name means grace or favor; blessings were on her life even in this difficult and trying time. God knew he could trust Hannah to follow through on the promise she made if God had given her a child. She had favor with God so when she prayed and was vulnerable with God, she was blessed to give birth to a baby boy whom she called Samuel because, "she [had] asked him of the Lord". She got exactly what she asked God for.

Ruth and Boaz is one of the most popular love stories in the Bible. I had a conversation with a friend from college about their story, what it meant, and how Boaz pursued Ruth. I thought it was rather interesting and I even surprised myself at what I got out of it because the story was not always this clear to me. Ruth became very close to her mother-in-law, Naomi, and she remained close even after the passing of her husband, father-in-law, and brother-in-law. As she was out in the field one day picking up leftover grain, Boaz spotted her and inquired about her. After finding out who she was, he told her to stay in his field and stay close to the women who worked for him. Boaz was immediately protective of her and cared for her. This was strange to Ruth, and honestly it was strange to me, too. Why would

LOVE FOR ALL THE WRONG REASONS

he be so protective and careful of her so soon? Boaz told her that he knew her story. In other words, her reputation had preceded her; he had heard about the kind of woman she was and he was able to see her value immediately. This is one thing we must consider when we are interested in dating.

On several occasions, it is quite possible for your demeanor to influence people's perception and ultimately help a man decide whether or not to pursue you. Given a detailed account of your past relationships, old habits, or track record, if you will, a man will pursue you based on what he wants at the time. If he has heard that you're promiscuous or "easy", and he is only interested in your bedroom skills, guess where he's headed? On the other hand, if he has heard that you are the epitome of what a wife should be and you know how to help make a man understand what you need and what you offer, and he's looking for a wife, guess where he's headed?

Boaz was obviously looking for a wife; otherwise he would have looked the other way when he saw this young lady in his field. He knew the potential in Ruth and as a "hunter," he decided to pursue her. Since her husband had died, Boaz was qualified to be her next husband. However, when Boaz knew that Ruth shared a mutual interest, he had to acknowledge that there was another man who was also qualified and he had to go about pursuing her the right way. Boaz had to see if the other man was willing to do his duty and marry Ruth. If the other man chose to acquire the land that belonged to their deceased relative, he would also acquire Ruth with it. For fear of harming his own estate, he told Boaz to redeem the land and Ruth. There was no hesitation on Boaz's part; he redeemed the land and married Ruth.

These two stories speak of the standards that we as women should set for ourselves. Elkanah had unconditional love and was not concerned with the scrutiny of their community because Hannah could not bear children. The foundation of their love was not built on favors or what they could give one another. In the case of Ruth and Boaz, Boaz followed the proper steps. You may have an interest in someone or even be in a relationship with someone who is just like the "other relative". He may not want to live up to your standards or make the sacrifice to be with you because of his own selfish reasons, but do not be discouraged because a man with the qualities of Boaz is smitten with you. He sees that the "other relative" is qualified, but he's not *willing*. The "other relative" obviously did not have the chance to see everything that Boaz saw in Ruth, and essentially, he just wasn't the right man for the job. Every man will not

LOVE FOR ALL THE WRONG REASONS

be willing to go to the lengths that Elkanah and Boaz went, but there is someone who is qualified *and* willing to take on the responsibility of loving and protecting you.

Love holds you accountable, brings out the best in you, and gives you the courage to love back. The right kind of love will help you understand why it took so much for you to get to this place and give you every bit of confidence in where you'll stay. I won't say it will make you complete because you should already be complete, but it will add a certain value to your life that makes it hard for you to understand how you ever lived without it. Love is not always easy, but it's always worth it, you just have to be willing to take the journey. Throughout the process, not only will you be a teacher, but you will also become a learner. You learn what your partner desires and you are given a better view of what you want and need for yourself. In the end, you can finally answer the question for yourself, what should love feel like?

LOVE FOR ALL THE WRONG REASONS

What Kept Me Going After Another Hit?

"How can I let some other woman enjoy all the hard work I put in for this man to get it right?" Honestly as I think about it more, that's how I really felt. I was the one who worked for five years to get him to understand me, to get him to want more for himself. There was one breakup before the final one that made me rethink a lot of things. I had put in so much work, and I had to question whether I was making the right decision by not going back, by not fighting for it. I didn't want to see my work being enjoyed by another woman. But it was in this moment that I realized that it's okay to get weak. You can judge me, but I'm being real. For a long time I've wanted him to value me and when he started to *sound* like he finally got it, it was hard for me to not even consider taking him back. The funny thing is I thought by the time he came back, I would have been strong enough to resist him and simply cut him off. Clearly that is not what happened.

I didn't have anything to say to him when he would call; I thought it was just to make sure I knew we were really over or to in some subliminal way, torture me

LOVE FOR ALL THE WRONG REASONS

because he knew I wasn't over him. We went back and forth for a while about why things went the way they did and what we should have done to make things right and have a normal, functioning relationship. Then he started to seem like the man I first met. He was being nice, consistent in conversation, relentless in trying to win me back. The only thing I kept thinking is that I've taken my heart back and it's in my protection until further notice because it doesn't seem like anyone else understands how fragile and important it is to me. I guess the burning question is, "Did you take him back?" Well…yes. I know, I know, judge me. The only thing I could think about was the many times that this has happened and the difference in this time. See, I loved this guy so much that every time we broke up I prayed and asked God to bring him back to me. This time I chose not to do that because in my mind there was no turning back. So without me praying for it, here he was, promising to do better and keep me happy. I figured we'd just have to see if he lived up to it this time. By no means did I proclaim to be perfect, and I've done wrong too, but I did believe he had a lot to prove, so this had to be destiny, right? We were meant to be together, right? Wrong.

My biggest challenge in this part of my story was dealing with the judgment. When we broke up he posted pictures on Facebook of himself and his new girlfriend saying that he hoped to get it right with her. So at this point, when people saw that we were back together, there's no telling what everyone would have to say. I kept asking myself, "Am I stupid or using poor judgment?" "Why couldn't I reject him the way I had planned?" Then I remembered my prayer that I had been praying for a long time. I asked God to guide me and keep me safe. If I accepted my ex back into my life, then there must have been something else God wanted from us. It was a major struggle because I felt like all my social media followers had a front row seat to my crazy story. Every breakup was obvious and every time we got back together it was obvious; it was also obvious that I looked stupid. Getting weak is not a crime, but in your weakness you have to search for your strength. I had to remember God's will for my life and not what everyone else felt I should do. Our story was unorthodox, confusing, and crazy…but it was just not over yet. It couldn't be over until I decided to make a change and grow; I had to be forced out of my comfort zone. I kept allowing him in until finally he hurt me in the deepest way.

We had been having a rough time dealing with the criticism from my parents and trying to decide what was best for the both of us. It became way too much for me to handle so I told him that we should go our separate ways. It was an unplanned, not well-thought out decision, but I said it. I regretted it immediately, but I just couldn't bring myself to take it back. I did not see any way for us to fix this situation and be happy together. After five years of going back and forth, three weeks after our last break up, invitations to his nuptials to someone else were being sent out! I could literally feel my heart break when I found out. Our breakups had never gone this far and I felt even more stupid than I had with every other breakup. Whom could I blame? Of course I blamed him in a major way. In three weeks he had decided to make a lifetime commitment to someone else? In my mind that could only mean one thing: he had had a relationship with her before we officially ended anything. Even though his decision was made and the damage was done, it was not easy for me to just accept it. I kept trying to make him see the stupidity in his choice, which was, once again, a mistake. My attempts were unsuccessful, and honestly, I'm glad they were.

You may say, "Well, you broke up with him. Why did it even matter to you what he did afterwards?" On the surface, that is a valid point, but breaking up does not mean my feelings for him were erased. If you stopped wearing a pair of shoes for a while, does it always mean you don't like them or want them anymore? No. In my heart I still wanted to work things out, I just didn't know how we could. Once again, considering the pattern that we had already created, I always thought there would be another chance. This time he moved quickly; he didn't just start a new relationship, he got married.

I had many conversations with his sister and even a couple with his dad about what was going on. When I first met his family, everyone made sure they told me to let them know if he wasn't doing right by me; but now that I look back on it, everyone knew it was a bad decision, and no one could stop him. No matter how much of a mistake he was making, or what his family said to me, when the wedding day came everyone was there with smiles on their faces and joy in their hearts. In fact, my cousin was the best man at his wedding. I felt betrayal and humiliation from all angles and I wanted to make him hurt just as much as he had hurt me. I didn't know how to do it, and I really didn't have it in me to do anything. In sensitive times such as this, you have to be careful because you can be so wrapped up in thinking that revenge is in your hands. At the end of the day, we cannot focus on what others are doing wrong; we have to focus on doing what we know is right, regardless of how we've been treated. It even had me wondering if God hated me. What did I do to deserve so much pain? Was I really that bad of a girlfriend? I had loved a man with all my heart and it seemed so easy for him to marry someone else.

I wanted to forget every single detail of this relationship, and I meant it. However, my best friend brought to my attention that if I forgot all of this, I would also lose the wisdom that I had gained in the process. Even then, I would ask, "Did I have to gain it *this* way?" I began to feel hate towards him and everything he stood for. I even found myself fostering horrible feelings toward some of his family. How could they have allowed him to be this stupid? Thoughts of suicide plagued me; questions of my worth haunted me; and fear that I would forever be in bondage because I loved him so much continued to pester me. For some reason, I always had this ounce of hope that he wouldn't repeat his pattern, but it never failed! So while he was preparing for a wedding to a woman he barely knew, I began writing this book.

I can admit that I started writing this book with bad intentions. I figured this would be the perfect opportunity to expose him and his family or talk trash about them to make myself feel vindicated, but because of couth and growth in both the spiritual and natural realm, I couldn't bring myself to do it. This growth did not occur overnight, though. Initially, I wouldn't have cared if a car had hit him; that's just how bitter I was. Karma is real and I knew she was definitely on her way to her next stop. There were no other words that I could use to describe the feelings I felt towards him except the fact that I couldn't wait for him to hurt as much as I was hurting. But whom does that help? No one. Don't get me wrong—that simple question did not immediately erase my feelings of anger and betrayal, but it helped me put my energy in a different place. I wanted to hate him, but it was clear that through this roller coaster I had to have hate for myself. I could not have loved myself if I allowed all of this to happen. Where was the consideration for myself? Where was the love? So it was time to start with me and put my chapter about Understanding You to good use. What did I really want? What did I need? Did I forgive myself for the things I've done or allowed? The answer is no. I let him back in time after time hoping that this time would be the time that we fixed it, or that we fixed each other. Saying, "We finally got it right." I would hope that five years of my life wasn't a waste, yet I felt it was, and it was made up of constant broken promises.

LOVE FOR ALL THE WRONG REASONS

I had to cope with myself and with the opinions of others once more. I remember hearing that my parents were the blame for all this happening because they shouldn't have allowed it to go this far. People made comments that suggested that I was overreacting. In regards to my cousin being his best man, I believe the comment was, "But that's his best friend…" as if that would to add a stitch to my broken heart. I was alone. Even though I got sympathy and people checked on me, it all felt like a horror movie. I was hurt, but some people thought I had no reason to be. I was angry, but some people thought I wasn't angry enough. I found myself attempting to feel what everyone else thought I should feel. I had to take a second look at the situation and figure out how to feel for myself. There is no one word that could describe how I felt, but if you didn't understand why it bothered me, you'd be happy to know I got over it.

In all this mess, there was a blessing. This one came through a baby girl named Kyla. My brother and his fiancé, at the time, were expecting a child (thankfully, it wasn't me; I'm not ready and I definitely would not have been ready to carry *his* child!). She was born two days before the wedding. What was so encouraging for me was when I looked up the meaning of her name and in the Hebrew language it means victorious! Victory was birthed from this terrible time; that had to be God's doing. I felt like I had so much love to give and now I had a positive place to put it. This introduced me to yet another kind of love. I was, and still am, excited about watching her grow and showing her the ropes in life. I want her to avoid heartbreak and recognize "game" when she sees it. Not only that, I want her to know that even without being able to say a word, she has been my motivation. Through her, I found strength to finish college and continue to go after my dreams even when so much seemed to be going wrong. Through her, I found a joy in life that I never knew existed. God created Kyla to show me that all hope was not lost and to give me the push that I so desperately needed. Love was starting to look all right again.

After being hurt, it is expected that one be guarded and defensive about your heart and whom you choose to let in. There is absolutely nothing wrong with that until the right people come into your life. What I'm basically saying is, don't block *everyone* out; trust your gut and use discernment. I remember when my ex first announced that he was getting married. I had been participating in an internship in Matthews, North Carolina and a guy that I had seen on multiple occasions sent me a message on Instagram. I thought it was strange because we had never even said two words to each other. Instead of starting our first encounter with a normal conversation, he wasted no time in asking what had happened between my ex and me. Since I knew he and my ex were acquainted, I thought this was some kind of underhanded scheme to get me to say something negative. Therefore, I was being guarded with this sudden surge of interest in my failed relationship. I gave him a careful answer by telling him my ex wanted to talk to my dad about us getting married, but was taking his time about doing it. Sensing that my ex was going to end it with me, I just told him that I didn't want to go through that anymore with him and less than a month later, my ex's announcing he's getting married. I held back every bit of rage and hurt that I could and chose my words wisely because I was so sure he was going to report back to my ex.

I could not have been more wrong about this guy. He never repeated our conversation and we've been really good friends ever since. In fact, he helped me see things in myself that I hadn't realized were there. I had to wipe the egg off my face because he had invalidated every preconceived idea I had about him. Sometimes we allow the hurt we experience to be the template we go by for every future relationship or friendship, causing us to ruin it before it even begins.

Over the next year, you wouldn't believe how much more there was for me to learn. Not long after I finally let my past go, I came back in contact with a young man who had an interest in me before, but we had never pursued a relationship. Initially, I just wasn't really interested and I thought he was way too old for me. This time, though, there was something that drew me to him like a magnet. I couldn't explain it, but I knew I wanted to see what had my heart jumping when I saw him for the first time in years. He looked the same, dressed the same, nothing had changed. So we started communicating and there was chemistry and evident attraction.

I was determined to make this experience different. I wanted to take my time and make sure I was ready to love with no reservations and not make him pay for the last man's mistakes. This was a long and necessary process. I had to remember that this wasn't the same man and try to avoid making him feel like I was comparing him to my ex. One mistake I believe a lot of people make is moving on too quickly in hopes that the next man or woman will be the hero to change your perspective and your whole life. It doesn't always work like that. Happiness is not in the next place, next relationship, or next person; it starts with *you*! You have to choose to be happy regardless of what happens.

Even though happiness is a choice, it's not always the *first* choice; therefore, if you are unhappy, you owe it to no one to make it seem as if you are. Too many times we focus on impressing others when in all actuality, they don't have it all together either. Covering up the truth doesn't help anyone. Just like everyone else, I have issues, and that's nothing to be ashamed of. While I was in the relationship with my ex, I relied way too much on him to help me define who I was and tell me what I'm capable of. The truth is, his opinion could do me no good and his words would only amount to a fraction of the magnitude of my abilities. I was, and am, capable of doing far more than he or even I could ever imagine. So it doesn't matter what people think about you. If everything is not going according to your plans, be confident in the simple fact that God's plan is always better. I did not "wake up like this" and I do not have it all together. It is not my responsibility to make *you* feel good about *me*.

I had to remind myself of this constantly because I was consumed with the trivial opinions of others. I was uncomfortable when people that knew what had happened looked at me too long. I felt like they were trying to figure out a way to show sympathy. When someone asked how I was doing and their tone was low and fatuous, I felt like they were asking out of pity. Everything started to bother me in the most inconsequential ways and it was driving me crazy. I knew with time that I'd get better and that this obstacle would pass, but I didn't want anybody to treat me differently because I was going through something.

Hiding the fact that something is wrong only makes it more difficult to rectify the situation. You cannot find the road to recovery if you refuse to acknowledge where you are. I'm not telling you to dwell on your current issues, but don't give off the impression that life is just picture perfect when it's just not so. If you are not happy, change your situation and don't let anyone make you feel guilty for doing so. That simple concept, along with my little niece watching my every move, and my God guiding my every footstep is what gave me the drive I needed to keep going. I couldn't quit because that was not the way for my story to end. I could not allow this hurt to take precedence over my purpose in life, and I had to be able to tell my story.

Even when the relationship was over, I felt like things were continuing to fall apart because I had made that man my world. Nothing went as I planned it. I wasn't satisfied and I had to ask myself, "Was I getting the punishment for *his* mistake?" No! I was learning yet another lesson. I had to learn to be content in whatever state I was in (Philippians 4:11, KJV). I received this confirmation while attending a vision board party hosted by my cousin, Audriana Smith. Harriet Huell Lampkin was the speaker. She is amazing! She told us her story, her accomplishments, and her many encounters with God that led her to this point in her life. There was a period in her life where she was unsure of where God's plan was taking her; she was in her "transitional phase".

After earning an undergraduate degree, some people have a hard time figuring out what their next move should be. It's hard to find a job, especially with no experience. When you finally get one you probably hate it and you might feel stuck, but she encouraged us to find peace in our struggles and learn to be content wherever God has sent you. Once you have decided to be satisfied, you have mastered that stage of your life. Being content does not mean you settle. Being content means you realize when you have what you need and you're just waiting on God to give you what you want. You don't give up praying for your heart's desires, but you gain a new level of appreciation for what you already have. This was a pivotal moment for me; it changed my whole perspective. My focus was showing gratitude for what I had and continuing to ask God in faith for what I wanted. Ms. Lampkin told us that once we have mastered the phase that God has us in, he pushes us into the next level. We have learned the lesson he prepared for us and now it's time for a new one. All of these lessons lead us to our purpose and destiny, even the things we don't like or understand.

I thought it was hilarious when I finally grasped what had happened with this relationship. With all the many breakups we had, I was being warned to let it go and since I wouldn't, God had to put me in a situation where I had no choice but to let go. The reason I could laugh about it was because I imagined how God may have reacted throughout the process. During each breakup God probably went from saying, "Finally these two understand that they shouldn't be together!" to "For real, girl? Y'all make my job hard." He had to be saying, "If she would just open her eyes to what I'm putting right in her face, she would run away from this boy. I have so much better for her." Through it all, though, I'm still grateful. When he saw that my own freewill was going to carry me down a road of regret, he stepped in and changed my direction. I prayed constantly for our relationship, hoping that we would get back together and it would get better. A lot of times it seems like God is doing the opposite of what we ask. We ask Him to fix the man we want the way we want him and he gets worse. We ask him for financial increase and get more bills instead. However, in each situation, God is growing us and showing us his power. I prayed for the right attributes, but he just wasn't the right man.

LOVE FOR ALL THE WRONG REASONS

Forgiveness and the Healing Process: It's All about You

Sometimes before someone even says a word you know they're not someone you want or need in your life. It is imperative for you to pick up on their vibes and not to ignore them. At the same time, you should remember that not everyone is out to hurt you. Some people are actually sent into your life to change it in a way that you never thought was possible. In developing new relationships and meeting new people, be careful not to treat them like the people who have left you or make them pay for other's mistakes. While it is actually disrespectful to your new friends, it's even more damaging for you. I found myself making unnecessary comparisons and doing the very thing I wanted to avoid doing. By making certain judgments I only showed that I wasn't ready; I wasn't over the relationship and it still hadn't occurred to me how much better I was or should be.

The measure of a relationship should not be based on things of the past; it could hurt the people you involve yourself with in the future. In simple terms, don't force yourself to remember the characteristics of the person who hurt you the most or completely turned your world upside down. There is absolutely nothing wrong with recognizing the traits that you know you don't want to deal with, but this shouldn't lead you to treat this new person how you *wish* you had treated someone from your past. You have to forgive yourself and forgive the person who hurt you. I would question the motives of my new love interest and fervently accuse him of things that he probably never did. It was easy for me to see what I thought was wrong before I even acknowledged what was right. I hadn't forgiven my ex and that made it hard on me and the person I was trying to move on with.

I would be lying if I said this was the easiest thing to do. In fact, this was the absolute hardest. It made absolutely no sense to me why someone would choose to hurt me this way, but it was done. Everyone has to cope with these types of situations in their own way, so I can only express what it took for *me* to get to this place. Initially, I went out of my way to avoid thinking about him or the situation. I didn't want to talk about him and if anyone mentioned him, I would be on the verge of tears. I would always try to hold back the tears because if they fell, I felt weak. I felt like I had given someone else the power to change my mood and that just wasn't me. After a while, it became easier to hear his name or think about all that I had gone through. I had to accept that all of it was not his fault. I was a part of the problem, too. I had allowed all of it to happen so before I could forgive him, I had to focus on me and give myself an honest examination. Who was I before I experienced this heartbreak? What were my values before I even met him? How had I changed for the better? How had I changed for the worst? Whom had I forgotten about?

All of this damage had to be assessed during the healing process, no matter how bad it was. In the damage assessment of a car, a mechanic runs tests, makes observations, and tells you how much it will cost and what it would take to fix your car. You need to go through the same process with your heart after it has been broken! If you try to drive the car before it's fixed, you could cause more damage and find yourself on the side of the road! Don't jump ahead of yourself; do the damage assessment. It will be a whole lot easier for you to have a healthy relationship with yourself and someone else. This process should not be constrained to a time limit. It's not a race, it's your heart.

It may take weeks, months, or even years, but that's okay. You deserve the chance to heal and rediscover who you are or who you want to be. You will appreciate this process more than you know because you will come to terms with reality and learn to accept it. Everyone gets hurt; it's inevitable, so in some way, someone has offended you before. Now in order to grow and move on, you have to forgive those who have hurt you. Otherwise, it just becomes baggage that you lug around with you and it shows in your relationships with people. However, one must remember that forgiveness is a process and although it may have taken a split second to hurt you, it could take much longer for you to get over it completely. That's okay, and don't let anyone convince you otherwise.

You owe it to no one to make it seem like you are okay with the way you have been treated. You owe it to no one to make yourself seem invincible or that your feelings can't be hurt. You owe no one. Those who mock your healing process by saying, "Oh my god, let it go. You should be over that by now," have no idea what it took for you to even get where you are right now. If you are still facing the situation, continue to heal on *your* time. You get impatient with yourself because if it's taking "too" long, you feel like people start labeling you as bitter. Let them.

While you're healing, take the time to evaluate every facet of the situation. Why were you offended? What were this person's intentions? How did you respond? How *should* you have responded? Have you told this person how they made you feel? Don't just hold on to it because you can. Give yourself the opportunity to really identify where and what the problem is so it can be resolved. This is for you, not anyone else. Forgive others so that it no longer takes up space in your life and so it does not become the template by which you judge other people. The progress you've made within yourself is far more important than what anyone thinks. This especially goes for the person who has caused the hurt; their opinion of your process is irrefutably insignificant. Your assignment is to forgive and that is all that can be asked of you.

We hold on to things for fear of not being able to find something better. If God didn't allow it to happen the way you had it mapped out in your head, I promise he has something better for you. Patience is a must even though it is one of the hardest attributes to practice. As humans, we have the tendency to go against the element of surprise. We can't wait to know what's going to happen; the suspense kills us and distracts us from the progress we could be making at that very moment. If you don't wait on God to reveal to you what he wants you to do, you could very well find yourself in another unpleasant situation.

LOVE FOR ALL THE WRONG REASONS

This is where your prayer life comes into play. You say you are ready and because you know who you are and what you need, you can ask God to give it to you. Through the healing process and understanding yourself, your perspective has changed. This prompts you to think clearly and critically about what will benefit you and contribute to your happiness.   The next relationship should be a contribution to, not creator of, your happiness. Be specific in your prayers and ask God to help you accept his will, no matter what it is. We pray for some things that are not always good for us in the long run. Thankfully, God can step in at any time and alter our situations and change our outlooks. My prayer whenever someone came into my life became, "Lord, show me his heart."   I wasn't too focused on his techniques of pursuing me, but more so his intentions after the pursuit slowed down. I needed to know that opening the door for the next person to come in wasn't going to be a waste of my time.

I wrote one specific prayer that I believe changed so much for me. I was at the point where I felt like taking my time in healing had done me so much good:

Dear Lord,

Thank you once again for the chance to talk to you. Lord there's some things I just can't seem to get off my mind. I

---

need your help, Lord. First I want to and have to thank you for allowing me to heal so well after being hurt so badly. Thank you for keeping my mind and fixing my heart. Thank you because you gave me the chance to get in touch with that part of you. If I had not experienced that hurt, I would not have this testimony. Now that I feel like I'm in a good space, I want to ask a favor of you. Send me my husband. When you do it, let me know within my heart that it's him. If it's someone I already know, please help me realize it and accept it. Open my eyes and heart so I don't ignore him or push him away. Help us both be prepared for a love like nothing we have ever experienced. Allow this love to be extraordinary and energizing. Let this love that we share show us why it could have never worked with anyone else. Help us create a space where only you and our relationship take up authority. Help us to be helpers to one another. Let this love light a fire in us that cannot be extinguished. Help us embrace one another in every flaw, stage, and phase of life. Don't let us run from each other, but run to each other and be each other's best friend. Every secret, every flaw, and every bit of shame, let it all be shared between us without one hint of judgment. Lord, help us to be faithful to each other at all times, resisting temptation and the penalties associated with them. Allow

LOVE FOR ALL THE WRONG REASONS

our hearts to intertwine in a way that makes us indescribably happy and at peace even if everything around us is falling apart. Let the attraction between us be so strong that even in a room full of beautiful women and handsome men, we only see each other. Help us to please you and each other. Allow us to impart wisdom to one another on a daily basis, encourage each other and be each other's strength, joy, and peace. Help us make each other's lives easier and let this love be right and strong. I'm not asking for it to make each of us complete, but let it add such value and excitement to our lives that we wonder how we ever made it without each other. Don't make us dependent on each other, but continue depending on you as the foundation of our friendship, relationship, and marriage. All these things I'm praying and believing for in Jesus' name
Amen.

     I believe that this prayer turned things around for me. At this point, I knew what I deserved and I had a new characterization of love. It's not only about how that person makes you feel, but it's about what they do for you. I don't mean materialistically; I mean what this person does for your heart. Sure, he or she can call you beautiful or handsome all day, but do your conversations make you think? Does your mate hold you accountable when you're wrong? Do you show each other strength even at your weakest point? Do you remind each other of your potential even when one of you feels like a failure? Love should balance you out and make up for what you lack. When you're together, there should be an insurmountable force to be reckoned with because there is nothing that the two of you can't accomplish together.

In order to truly heal, you have to face situations and issues about yourself that make you uncomfortable. This helps you figure out more about who you are. I had to come to grips with the fact that I was not happy with who I was. I would look at other people coming into themselves and really embrace who they are and I was just on the sideline waiting…I don't know exactly what I was waiting for, though. I was proud of all my peers for finding themselves, but I struggled with the process. After I graduated from college, I felt more lost and alone than ever. I had no clue how to live my life and I thought everyone could see that. It took me a while to find a job and when I finally did, I hated it and resigned after training. I had interview after interview, but the job I finally got didn't even require me to have an interview! God and my aunt looked out for me on that one. Even with a job, I felt I was an underachiever. Not only was life after college a little difficult; I was not happy with

LOVE FOR ALL THE WRONG REASONS

what I saw when I looked in the mirror. I was having trouble with my weight, my forehead seemed to be getting larger by the minute, and I felt like I had big man-looking hands. In hindsight, it was stuff that did not even matter. I was always finding something wrong or comparing myself to other women and I couldn't help it. I had to figure out how to get over this hump. So I started digging deeper and finding ways to love myself in a better way. I started focusing on why God even loves me. Through his eyes, I am more than a conqueror. I am enough. He loves me in spite of all my flaws and blesses me regardless of all my mistakes. If God can love me through *anything*, then I can love myself through anything, too.

Taking into consideration that life and death lie in the power of my tongue (Proverbs 18:21, KJV), I had to speak life over myself until I got better. With each passing day, you will start to believe the words you speak more and more. Speak healing over yourself by saying, "I am healed. I am whole. I am worthy of love." Evaluate yourself regularly in forgiving yourself and others, and understanding how you got to this point. Ask yourself hard questions like, "If I got into a relationship today, would I be able to trust him? Would I constantly and unnecessarily compare him to my ex? Do I still focus on how I was treated?" Keep up with things like this so you know when you're ready to let someone else in.

Through the course of the relationship, I had become a dependent, passive, and reserved girl–the total opposite of what I was before. I changed who I was most times to avoid arguments and essentially to keep him. I wanted him to be able to brag about how good of a girlfriend I was to him. I hated confrontation so I just let things go to avoid talking about problems. If I felt disrespected, I would seldom express it to him and silently deal with it myself. I didn't want to lose him so I tried to compromise every part of my life to make sure he was comfortable. Now that all of it is over, I can see where I went wrong. I have given myself time for reinvention and renovation. I am comfortable with who I am and I have to thank God for allowing me to experience all of this. My confidence in myself is back and I am no longer allowing anyone to change who I am. You either take me as I am, or leave me where I am. Mediocrity is a thing of the past and it no longer has a place in my life. I realized how unhealthy it was for me to foster all of that resentment and avoid confrontation. So now when I have a problem, it is addressed. If we can't work through it and resolve it, I have no problem ending the relationship. I have more respect for myself now than ever before because I now know just how strong I am and who I am.

My relationship with God has gotten even better. Anyone who comes into your life should increase positivity and bring you closer to God. I am inspired to grow in God and get to know Him more than I ever have. God has shown me that it's always worth another shot. Even if a relationship doesn't last, it is all a part of God's strategic plan. Sometimes he chooses to give you a taste of what you asked for just to show you that it's not what you need. I wanted so badly to be married and happy with my ex, but God showed me in his own perfect way that that was not what I needed. It is because of this, and many more reasons, I can say that I have forgiven myself and I've never been happier. Every day I still wonder how in the world I let things get that far, but along with that thought also comes the appreciation that I have for the lessons I learned throughout the entire process.

Trust the process because like every other thing in life, "this, too, shall pass." That quote applies to good times and bad times because Ecclesiastes 3:1 tells us, "To every thing there is a season, and a time to every purpose under the heaven:" then in verse 6 it says, "A time to get, and a time to lose; a time to keep, and a time to cast away." I knew within myself that this was going to be a slow, steady process and every single day was a purge for me. The first day there was a sacrificial burning ceremony for all the things my ex bought me and wrote for me. All of it had to go. I cried for hours and I remember my dad telling me, "Get it all out. Don't let it drive you crazy." I don't remember when, but at some point I deleted my ex from any social media accounts that I actually paid attention to. All communication stopped between me and anyone he was connected to, including any of my own family members. Finally, I just let the healing happen. Every time something reminded me of him, it got easier to deal with it. I no longer looked at it as a waste of time or a painful memory; it became my story and purpose and a part of my developing identity. I thought I was grown, but I was still growing and definitely still learning.

As far as forgiving him, I believe I have. I've heard people say the best way to know if you've forgiven someone is if you would help them after they've done you wrong. I would help him and his wife. I don't want them to need me for anything; in fact, I'd rather not have any contact with him. However, if the day comes where I can help them and they ask, I will. I forgive him, even if he's not sorry. I forgive his family for justifying his wrong towards me. I even forgive my cousin for what I felt like was betrayal to me by participating in the wedding. I forgive so I can be free and remain free. Forgiving him means he has no more power over my life; he no longer has a place of comparison in my relationships. He is no longer the template to any future relationships I may have. I will not say he no longer matters because it was through him that I've learned so many valuable lessons and I was able to find my purpose and testimony. I can inspire others and evade the possibility of a developing pattern myself.

No sooner than I confessed it with my mouth was I tested on it. He contacted me for the first time in a long time and I found it extremely strange. He apologized for everything, including turning me into a cold woman. It was very nice of him and I appreciated it, but I didn't *need* it anymore because I had already made up in my mind that he was forgiven. I was not expecting an apology and even though I got one, I was going to be perfectly fine without one. You will be satisfied in knowing that you've done all you can, so don't expect apologies! Sometimes people prefer not to be given an apology based on the pretense that it may not even be genuine. So be content even with the apology you didn't get. He or she may not apologize, but trust me, they're sorry.

You'd think that after all he put me through, I'd reject the chance to say two words to him, but I don't. Despite what people may think, you can have a decent or cordial relationship with someone who has hurt you. This does not mean you have to become best friends, but it means you chose to show the love of Jesus in your actions. How many times do you disappoint or disregard God? How many times did he forsake you? See my point? I forgave this man and many others who have done me wrong. I refuse to show bitterness and hatred towards anyone, including him. When I heard people talk negatively about him or how he had hurt me, I'd brush it off by telling them, "I'm over it now. Let's talk about something else." He was wrong, but constantly criticizing him and reliving the situation would not help. I'm sure by now he knows things could have been done differently. Not long after that, his church temporarily became closely affiliated with where I worship. So seeing him and his family throughout the year was an adjustment I was going to have to make, grudgingly, nonetheless an adjustment.

For me, forgiving him means treating him like nothing happened. He will never hold the same place he once held in my heart, but I will not allow triviality to consume me. He was wrong, Stevie Wonder could see that, but for me to treat him just as badly would only reflect on me. At the conclusion of it all, I have to be at peace with myself. By no means am I suggesting that this will be an easy fix—you have to be willing to do the work. In the end, make sure you can honestly say you love yourself, you've accepted the part that you played, and you've learned valuable lessons. Forgiveness is such a powerful and emancipating experience. You take back your power and see the blessing that was hidden in all of the turmoil; it's the ugliest ordeals that give us the most beautiful testimonies. In my mind, I thought God was testing me just to see if I would say something offensive or do something that would totally misrepresent him and the forgiveness that I felt I had for him. I think I passed.

LOVE FOR ALL THE WRONG REASONS

One Template Is Not the Only Template

Giving you advice about how to overcome a terrible breakup or discover just how valuable you are does no good if I don't practice what I preach. After all I went through with my ex, I just knew God wasn't going to let me get hurt again. I thought, "Okay, this has to be it because I can't take anymore." Remember the new love interest I mentioned earlier? Of course there's a story with him, too. At first, he was doing all the right things. There was lots of attention, phone calls, and outings, everything that made me feel special. He even inspired me to grow in my relationship with God. Then I noticed a few things that bothered me. He would stop answering text messages, we would barely talk throughout the day, and things were just awkward for me. Conversing throughout the entire day is not a requirement, but if you start one way, then I believe you should continue that way.

Since I knew that he was a busy man, I thought I was just overreacting and I adjusted myself to it; I made myself think it wasn't a big deal. As time went on, we continued to communicate and I grew to like him a lot.

The first bomb dropped about a month after we had been talking. I was in town and we met up at the mall (It wasn't a date; we just really wanted to see each other). I noticed that he kept bringing up dating men with children and he wanted to know how I felt about it. I didn't have a problem with it, especially if the guy was taking care of his children, and the mother of the children understood that he was moving on. He kept bringing it up so I said, "Why do you keep asking me about kids? Do you have kids?" He looked at me with the most pitiful eyes and that gave it all away. A woman he had been with before me was about two months pregnant and he had just found out on his birthday.

I had to absorb all that rather quickly and really think about what I should do. I couldn't hold it against him because that was something that happened before we began talking. So I asked basic questions like, "Are you sure the baby is yours?" and "Do you love her?" I had to make sure I didn't willingly agree to looking stupid. I didn't judge him and I continued to work towards a relationship with him because I honestly thought it was worth it. As time passed, I would ask him if the mother of his child knew about me and that he was working towards a relationship with me. He would minimize the importance of the question by saying she didn't need to know his business and the only thing they talked about was the baby. It completely offended me and it didn't matter to him because as far as I knew, she still didn't know about me. I contemplated having my own conversation with her, but that would have been against my better judgment. There was no need to start any drama or make things worse.

Not long after he found out he was going to be a father, he lost his job. It sent him into a frenzy because he knew he couldn't take care of his responsibilities without a job so I tried to help him find another one. I let him use my laptop and we would sit there and search for jobs together. I even put in applications for him when I saw a job that would be good for him. He finally got one, but he didn't like it. He had my support and he quit and found another one. He stayed on that job for about four months and got fired. During the time I had been hearing that I wasn't the only female he was pursuing. I couldn't get too upset because we weren't officially in a relationship, but that was precisely the problem. He would tell me that's what we were working towards, but all the signs pointed in the opposite direction.

Finally he told me it just wasn't the right time for him and you wouldn't believe the reason why! He was still trying to get over one of his exes! That was something that he should've disclosed at the *beginning*, not the *middle*! By that time I had begun to fall in love; I wasn't deep, but I was getting close. My intuition kept telling me there was something I was going to get out of this so I had to stay. Affection started to get scarce and I was getting worried. Instead of just letting things die, I tried to do small things to show affection. I even wrote him "Open When" letters. On each envelope it had messages like, "Open when you want to know why I fell in love with you" or "Open when we've had an argument". In some way, each of them gave him written instructions on how to love me, what I liked, who I am, and who I thought he was and how I admired him. To this day, I have no idea if he even read them or if he even kept them. It just continued to go downhill and I was thinking, "Was I really about to get hurt *again*?" To guard my heart, I stopped trying as hard. I didn't force conversations with him, and I put my mind on other things and people. Then Thanksgiving Day came. He was invited to come to my home and as a matter of fact, he volunteered to come! I was thinking it would be a good experience and a move in a positive direction for us. I had never had anyone over for Thanksgiving so I was extremely excited, and I helped cook and set everything up, wanting it to be perfect.

LOVE FOR ALL THE WRONG REASONS

On Thanksgiving Day, he sent me a message and said that they had to rush his mom to the emergency room. I thought this was a major coincidence, just like every other time something was wrong with his mom or something came up when he was supposed to visit. Because it was so serious, I just knew he wouldn't lie about something like that, so I let my family know what was going on and we prayed for his mom. Even though it was a dire situation, my intuition just kept saying, "No, honey. He's lying." The next day I sent a text to his brother and asked if the hospital had kept his mom overnight. He was completely lost and told me somebody had lied to me. I was completely disgusted. How could someone make up that kind of lie? When I confronted him about it, he still tried to maintain his composure until there was no way he could deny it. He then told me that one of his friends was in a car accident and he had to rush to North Carolina. He didn't want me to feel like I was second to anything, but now I wonder if I was ever in the numbering.

There's no happy ending to this, it just gets worse. His friend was not in a wreck because one of my friends contacted him and he was fine. While I was explaining what had happened to one of my closest friends, he confirmed that the guy had not even been in North

Carolina because he saw him in Kingstree, South Carolina. I was past trying to figure out if it was worth fighting for. If he can make up a lie that big about something so small, there was no telling what else he could come up with. How could I trust someone like that? So my intuition was right in a sense because I did get something out of this: even people with religious titles can mess up. You guessed it, he was a minister! I thought since he had such a heavy responsibility, he wouldn't sabotage his reputation by being so foul. I was wrong. I can set expectations and firm standards, but I can't automatically assume that he will be the perfect match because of who he is supposed to be and what he is supposed to represent. After a year of being single, I thought it was long enough and I could handle dating again, but I sure didn't think *that* would be my *first* experience. I still had faith that it would get better because it sure couldn't get worse.

Now that I have taken a few steps back, I can see how he was always in control. He controlled the very fact that we weren't in a relationship, and he even controlled when we saw each other. Whenever we went to restaurants, he would ask for specific seating. Each time the seats were in isolated areas, but I didn't make a fuss about it because he did that whether we were by ourselves or with a group. All of these should have been mutual decisions. A select group of people knew we were communicating on that level, and we never even gave hints on social media. *Everyone* doesn't have to know, but if *no one* does, then where are the boundaries? When and how could I hold him accountable? For all I knew, he could be having identical conversations with several females and because we were completely clueless of one another, we'd think we were the only ones. Everyone is so caught up in this trend about not needing a title. Honestly, you don't *need* one, but I see this as another way for a dishonest person to evade commitment. When I say, "That's my man," it alludes to the responsibilities and rules of that title. So to avoid those responsibilities, people settle for "situationships". If I'm not called anything more than a friend, I cannot expect to be treated any differently than such. Make it known who and what you are to each other so there are no blurred lines and hurt feelings.

The problem was I couldn't see how bad the situation was because I was focused on avoiding anyone with the same characteristics as my ex. I was falling in love only because I thought he was the complete opposite of my ex…the wrong reason. I didn't pay attention to the fact that that's not the only kind of man that exists. There

LOVE FOR ALL THE WRONG REASONS

are different types of stupid and my ex only showed me one. There are men who are completely clueless when they have a good woman, men who are habitual liars, ones who only want to pursue you to prove that they can have you, and the list could go on. However, there are also men out there who want to prove that they are not like the others, ones who only want to love you the way you deserve to be loved, but you have to be ready for them and love them back for all the right reasons.

I had his words inscribed in my head about not making him pay for the last man's mistakes so much that it made me blind to what was actually happening. The last man's mistakes replayed over and over in my mind and since they were so different, I couldn't recognize the danger right in front of me. I was subliminally compelled to caress his ego quite often. He would say things like, "I feel less than a man" or "I'm all right. I can do better." I didn't like hearing him say things like that so I would always make sure he knew how amazing I thought he was. I felt like encouraging him and pouring into his spirit was a part of my job; I didn't realize it would drain me. As much as I pushed him and tried to make him see his own potential, it wasn't reciprocated. Of course, I would get the occasional, "You're beautiful," "You're amazing", but it felt like a mere sip compared to the gallons I was pouring into him.

Instead of looking for an opportunist, I should have been made aware of the habitual liar and the "Mr. Intentional" I had come in contact with. We can't focus so heavily on what the last person did to us that we ignore what the next person *could* do to us. I'm not telling you to look forward to getting hurt, but I am telling you that no one is perfect and they could hurt you whether it's intentional or not. One template is not the only template and sometimes we as women can't recognize a good man even if he throws rose petals in our faces. Maybe it stems from past relationships or lack of a good father figure, but whatever the case may be, it has caused damage and it should lead us to do the damage assessment.

The Single Life

"Girl, you're going to be so lonely." "You still don't have a man?" I have a different eye roll for every myth and opinion that comes along with being single. Being single does not mean you're lonely! Do not allow yourself to succumb to what others believe about your life. Most times the same people who make such imprudent statements are the same ones wasting their time in toxic, unhealthy relationships, simultaneously wishing they had your life. Oftentimes, these are the same people who have chosen to work on relationships that have weak foundations and were destined to fail from the start. Some are even staying in relationships for sexual satisfaction. Staying in a relationship because of what someone can do in the bedroom is one of the most unfulfilling things you can do. Being in a relationship is not the end all, be all of life. When you're single there's so much less (or more) you have to think about.

Having a companion, someone to listen to you ramble about your day, and take you out every once in a while does bring a huge amount of value and excitement to your life, though. For those reasons, I can't say that I didn't *want* to be in a relationship. After a year of being single, I actually thought I was ready for something real.

LOVE FOR ALL THE WRONG REASONS

So I got a little impatient and honestly I felt like I was getting desperate. My friends were in what seemed to be good relationships and nobody had much time for me. I wanted a man; it was getting frustrating. I would put my phone down for hours and come back to no messages or missed calls. I longed for someone to want and need me. For the longest time, I felt like I was experiencing a drought because every guy that did try to pursue me didn't meet the criteria. Every guy was either ugly or too ugly to be as conceited as they were, didn't have enough ambition, or showed that all they were willing to do was play games from the very beginning. Every guy that I thought was attractive paid me no attention and I just could not understand it. It was like God decided to blind every guy that I had an interest in and watch me squirm for their attention. Why did I have to wait any longer?

The answer is quite simple: I was not ready. We have to remember that God is strategic in all he does so I had to trust the process. We may not like it or understand why, but it will make us better. What was even more important for me to understand was that every guy I encountered did not have to be considered as a romantic partner. Contrary to popular belief, I believe men and women can have strictly platonic relationships. I had to come in contact with my "Mr. Intentional" so that I could

LOVE FOR ALL THE WRONG REASONS

eventually find "Peace of Mind" and truly appreciate it as Miss Lauryn Hill would sing. Mr. Intentional knows just what to say. He has a way of making you feel like the only one who matters. You know, like Miss Lauryn Hill said, his words are "seasoned to perfection." Soon enough you start depending on his every word and seeking his validation. You confuse his humility with the "need to be needed" because he says, "No, I'm not that great." You find out eventually that he's conceited. Conceited, being an understatement because in his mind, he's God's gift to women.

By this time you're racking your brain trying to figure out how you got to this dead end. The answer is simple, "He says there's no me without him…" and you believed it. Thankfully, your senses found you after you left them at your first encounter with him. You pick them up and put him down, giving yourself the chance to find peace of mind. Here you are, finally in love and discovering the "meaning of a lasting relationship, not based on ownership." It's beautiful isn't it? I'm not saying you find this meaning in a relationship with another man; you find it with yourself *first*. I am more than grateful to have encountered my Mr. Intentional. I learned valuable lessons on how to "peep" game and protect my heart. With no opacity in my vision, I can see

Mr. Right strolling in equipped with a beautiful smile and the soul to match; he has every intention to treat me like a queen (slight pun intended). He sees that I'm priceless and is more than ready to capture my heart. If I had not met those clueless Mr. Intentionals, it would have been difficult for me to recognize him and the differences that separate them. So we all need at least one Mr. Intentional to learn from, but don't make this a habit. Mr. Intentional has all the same tricks and intentions, just different faces. It's a beautiful journey now that I think about it, and I wouldn't have had it any other way.

God had to be showing me everything I thought I wanted so I would know exactly what I needed. It was through this phase that I wanted to know what other people thought of love, specifically males. Maybe I was looking at love the wrong way or perhaps I didn't know what it actually meant. Did it mean the same thing to men as it did to me? Well, I decided to ask some of my closest male friends what they thought love meant. I didn't want anything generic like, "The deepest emotion you can feel for someone." I wanted them to give opinions that would send chills down my spine and make me alter my own perception.

In a sense, I needed to reassure myself that there still are some men who take love seriously and know how

LOVE FOR ALL THE WRONG REASONS

powerful it really is. I needed this reassurance because obviously the men I had dealt with on that level ignored the purity and peace that is love. Had I overestimated its value? Was I just a whole lot more mature than my male counterparts? I believe it was the latter and I arrived at this conclusion when I really began to understand and embrace myself and how I love. Stephon told me that the measure of a woman's love is much greater than a man's. He also told me that it is easy for a man to love a woman when she's strong and supportive and has a view of the future. However, when asked about what makes a woman love a man, he had a different emphasis on that process. It was as if he had anticipated the question. In his opinion, a man should be a woman's rock, respect her, and have her best interests at heart. His view on love was mostly about finding a support system in one another.

When I asked Nigel, there was no hesitation for him. He said, "Love is reflective of God. Love is not just an emotion but also an action that doesn't give up, doesn't bend and doesn't break. Love is found when one becomes vulnerable." His perspective put emphasis on foundational aspects of a relationship and how important it is to stay together. So far I felt like I had the right idea of what love meant so it made me wonder how I ever

LOVE FOR ALL THE WRONG REASONS

ended up with the guys who were clueless. I asked Carlton and he made it simple, "Internal expression where you can't imagine life without a certain individual." It was clear that we all knew the significance of such a potent feeling, so maybe my idea of it wasn't so wrong; maybe I just went about it the wrong way. Sometimes doing everything the way you think is right still isn't good enough. So now what?

I had to wait. Rushing things would only have made it worse for me because it would have put me in the position to fake like I was completely healed even if I wasn't. We find ourselves in compromising situations and then we expect God himself to come down and get us out of them. Sometimes we ignore the signs that he gives us at the very beginning. We have to use discernment and the common sense that God has already given us. We can avoid some hardships by taking things slowly and consulting God before making any final decisions. In my waiting process, there were opportunities to develop romantic relationships, but I knew it wasn't time for me. The funny thing is some guys approach you expecting you to continue a conversation like you owe them something. I'm not saying you should be rude to them, but be wary of the vibes you entertain and the impressions you give off.

LOVE FOR ALL THE WRONG REASONS

Sometimes we welcome in, or attract, the very thing we want to avoid because we have not changed ourselves. We don't want a man that we have to raise, but we *accept* a man that needs to be raised. We don't want a man that has no ambition, yet we *accept* a man whose biggest and most prevalent goal is to beat his friends on Madden 2k17. It doesn't add up and it sure won't multiply into happiness. I didn't want a man that didn't automatically recognize my value, yet I *accepted* men who took me for granted. So I waited, and I have learned in my waiting that things are so clear when you have no one clouding your judgment. It's comical how life can turn you upside down just so you can see what's been right in front of you the whole time.

Almost every female has that one guy that she should've given a chance to. We just chose to ignore him because at the time he just didn't have what we think we needed, or maybe we thought he was not even interested. A lot of times we couldn't have been any further away from the truth. Being single definitely allows you to explore your options. There are occasions where God places people in your attention before he places them in your path. You may notice someone and how amazing you think they could be before they become an actual part of your life. For example, I had met a guy that I thought was very talented and had good intentions. I quickly assumed that I just wasn't his type when I first met him. Later I began to communicate with him and found out that he was actually interested, but there still was no rush to get in an official relationship. The previous experience showed me that I wasn't quite ready for it, and I was okay with that.

Being single also gives you plenty of time to reflect. This is a vital part of healing, and if it is not done thoroughly, you can easily repeat the same mistakes from previous relationships. Even though there were several bad occurrences that had plagued my life over the past year and a half, there still was some good. We all know bad days make you appreciate the good days even more, and my life was the embodiment of that phrase. I was able to see what *could* have happened if I had followed through on my plan, and I was able to see what I was protected from.

In situations such as mine, where you've given your all only to be disappointed, it is quite possible to find someone who is in a state of depression or insanity. I've heard stories of women who lost their minds over a man or just completely gave up on life because of what they went through with a man. Thanks to God, that's not me. God kept my mind! Even though I had those

LOVE FOR ALL THE WRONG REASONS

thoughts, they were never put into action, and for that I am eternally grateful.

While I was trying to get over the situation, I thought the easiest way to heal was to avoid it altogether by killing myself or hurting someone else. When I say kill myself, I mean it in two different forms. Of course there's the literal option of committing suicide, but you can also kill yourself by cutting ties with everyone and everything. I thought that avoiding interactions with anyone else, making myself seem nonexistent, and essentially becoming the Walking Dead could save me a lot of embarrassment and pain. If I chose to become a hermit, then there would be no way anyone could cause me any pain, right? I chose the hard way out by choosing life in spite of all that had happened. I did not choose it because I wanted to, but because I needed to. This was something that I had to face head on so that I would not allow it to consume the rest of my life and all the aspirations I had for myself.

Excluding myself from the world would not make this unfortunate set of events disappear. In fact, it may have made it harder to heal. As a result of having people around me who care about me and want to see me heal, it made it easier to do. Without them, this process would have been much longer and harder. I couldn't avoid having conversations about it or seeing the posts on social media because in the most gentle and harmless way, they brought it up. It wouldn't be with malicious intent, but I imagine each time they did, it was an assessment of where I was in the healing process. This is why you need genuine people in your corner. Whether you want to or not, they push you to face yourself and your issues. I will always give credit to my friends and my family for helping me throughout this process because they accomplished more than they know. Through them I discovered new ways of looking at my situation and a stronger awareness for the strength that lies within me.

While you're in this stage, I think it is also a good idea to get reacquainted with some people. No, not your exes; they should remain exes unless a miracle occurs. Let's start with God. Sure, we all say we know him, but do we really? Now would be the perfect time to establish the relationship you *should've* had with him. Take time out to read the Bible, get more familiar with the ways of God and what he requires from you. Use other credible sources to translate the Bible if you are unsure about what is being said in the scriptures. This will help you increase your faith in Him and understand why He has allowed you to go through certain trials. Sometimes we have trouble trusting Him simply because we don't understand Him. You will never know the thoughts of God, but by reading and understanding His Word, you will begin to comprehend the purity of his actions. If at any time you feel discouraged, just read Jeremiah 29:11, "For I know the thoughts that I think toward you, saith the Lord, thoughts of peace, and not of evil, to give you an expected end" (KJV). Reading Romans 8:28 is always helpful when you need to be reminded of his goodness. It says, "And we know that all things work together for good to them that love God, to them who are the called according to his purpose" (KJV).

Throughout this time in my life, my faith was meticulously and constantly tested, and I felt like I had failed every time. Guilt weighed in on me because I was asking the question, "God, where are you?" as if He had ever left me. That, to me, was the personification of not trusting God. Ironically, this is how I got to know Him. Prayer was my release because after talking to God everything felt okay. I didn't realize how much of a comforter He was until I needed comforting. I had no clue how much of a heart fixer He was until mine was broken. There was no way I could know how much of a mind regulator He was until I felt like I was losing mine. In order to get to know Him, from time to time He has to put us in a state of uncertainty and austerity, which shows us that God is our only hope. Those trying times will cause you to know Him in ways you never thought of and make you stronger than you can imagine.

After you have reconnected with God, reconnect with yourself. Those hobbies or projects that you didn't have time for anymore because you were focused on your relationship are waiting for you to revive them. Now you can take your time and perfect them and make yourself proud. Identify your flaws and assess whether or not they can be changed or if you even want to change them. For example, I over analyze things *all the time*. I'm sure I'm not alone on that, but I did it so much that it wore my mind out so I had to change this. As a result of my becoming better communed with God, it became easier for me to say, "Lord, it's in your hands." I was able to eliminate unnecessary stress and be a happier person. Your flaws can be big or small; it's up to you to decide whether they continue to exist. Remember any promises you made yourself that you weren't able to keep. Start over. Give yourself a chance to follow through with what was obviously important to you. I promise you're not the only person who has broken promises because I know I've broken vows that I've made to myself. I promised myself that I would no longer hold on to people that

LOVE FOR ALL THE WRONG REASONS

obviously didn't want to hold on to me. Obviously, I broke that promise when I allowed people to use me as a doormat, and it caused me a lot of heartache. If you have to recommit yourself to abstinence, do it. There is absolutely nothing wrong with waiting for marriage to have sex. You will have a clearer idea of who the person is on a mental level. This is better because falling in love with their mind and soul can keep you in love even if their looks and sex drive fade away. We will get to a place where sex is not all we are looking for. There has to be something with substance that helps us stay in love with someone. If he or she cannot respect your decision to wait, then it would be hard not to draw the conclusion that sex is what they want from you. You may have gotten weak, but repent and get forgiveness from the Lord and forgive yourself. Whatever it is, you can do it!

There may have been some friendships that you allowed to dissolve, not because either of you were being a bad friend, but because they were hindering your relationship. Maybe they were requiring too much of your time or attention and you weren't willing to give it to them because of your own selfish reasons. It's possible that they were in opposition of your relationship so you decided that it would be best if you weren't friends anymore. The bottom line is, your friend was

LOVE FOR ALL THE WRONG REASONS

probably telling the truth and it wasn't what you wanted to hear. Swallow your pride and apologize so that you can begin to restore the relationship. Fix it; allow yourself to be vulnerable enough to admit that you were wrong and be willing to do what it takes to repair the friendship. More often than not, when you have had a real friendship, your friend will be just as willing as you to rebuild what the both of you had.

Being in a relationship or getting married is not a race and it's not the only goal you should have. Some of the best marriages took a lot of time to develop. Each stage of life is simply what you make of it. If you allow being single to be associated with discontent and loneliness, that's exactly what it will be for you. Thus, being single is a sensitive and evolutionary time and you should enjoy it because you'll miss it. You're allowed to feel every emotion and not be judged for it. However you feel in each moment is the exact way you are supposed to feel because no one can tell you exactly what it will take for you to be okay. You're able to grow and become one with yourself again and determine what will make you completely satisfied when it is time for another relationship. At this point, you can say that you've learned a lot about yourself and you start to focus more on what you need than what you want. Trivial things

LOVE FOR ALL THE WRONG REASONS

start to seem even more insignificant than before, and you realize what your soul craves is deeper. By now, you should be able to love yourself and your own company more than anyone else's. The next person that you let in should make you feel like their presence is more pleasant and necessary than being alone. When you have gotten in touch with that part of yourself, you tend to have less tolerance for anything that does not reflect what your soul needs. It is then that you can begin to love for all the right reasons.

LOVE FOR ALL THE WRONG REASONS

Your Next Relationship

You've reconnected and improved, so it should be time for another relationship, right? Sure, but maybe not as soon as you expect. With a deeper understanding of what you need and your new set of standards, you could find yourself turning away many suitors before you meet one that you think is worth your time. Not only that, people may be rejecting you because you are ready for something more than what they are willing to give. In either circumstance, you have to learn to cope with it and successfully move on. This is all a part of the process and road to discovering the right reasons to love. Since you took the time to properly heal and see things clearly, you automatically "peep" game before he even has the chance to play you. This time, instead of getting your heart broken, you're better able to protect and preserve it. This may take a while and you have to be willing to wait for it.

It could be that no one is even approaching you with the intention of becoming better acquainted or developing a relationship, but you have to ask yourself why? Do you go places that will give men or women the opportunity to approach you? Do you present yourself as friendly? You may not always find someone on the

LOVE FOR ALL THE WRONG REASONS

internet; leave the house! Get dressed and go to local events, window shop at the mall, or even try a new art or cooking class. When Naomi, Ruth's mother-in-law, found out about Boaz, she told Ruth to clean herself up and get her man. Maybe she didn't say it like that, but that was the gist of it. Ruth wasn't going to get Boaz by staying in the house; she had to be seen. There are men and women out there and they are not all sitting behind their computer screens. You have to be willing to put yourself on the market, but your price tag should say, "Priceless". Make yourself available, but not desperate. This is the kind of advice I had to consider for myself! When you feel like you're ready, you think it is okay to scope out your options and simply get in a relationship. You can, but it's much easier said than done. I can admit to this because I was saying, "Well I'm ready. These dudes are taking too long." Then one day I was scrolling down my timeline and I saw this beautiful man playing the saxophone. It was the best I had ever heard, but I may be biased. I was immediately attracted to him, of course, and I wanted so badly for him to notice me. He didn't.

Isn't that always the case, though? The guys that we find attractive and want to know more about are the main ones that bypass our inboxes. Unfortunately, the

LOVE FOR ALL THE WRONG REASONS

ones that we try so hard to avoid are the bold little soldiers who find it irresistible to invade our inbox with the typical misspelled words and mundane conversation. Since he either didn't notice me or was too shy to say anything, I took it upon myself to send him a message. No, I didn't try to "holla;" I just had a short and sweet conversation to make him see me. One conversation doesn't always add up to an automatic developing friendship, so I couldn't go in with that expectation. After that conversation, we didn't talk unless I initiated it. So I made a decision. He obviously had no interest in having a conversation with me, so I stopped. There was no need for me to make a fool of myself by constantly starting unwanted conversations. At least that's what I thought. I stepped out of my comfort zone and felt extremely uncomfortable, but what did I lose? Nothing; I accepted it and kept moving. Unfortunately, I made this decision *after* I made a commitment to come to one of his shows the following month. Go figure.

So I saw him for the first time in person at Bricktown Bistro and Bar in Columbia, SC. Briana and I got there about 30 minutes early so we sat in the car talking for a little while. As we sat there, I observed my surroundings. I spotted his car and a few minutes later he came running out to the car. For a second he was all I

LOVE FOR ALL THE WRONG REASONS

could see. He grabbed his shirt and jacket and went back inside, but not before a young lady came out behind him. I thought, "Ah, crap. Well…wait maybe that's his sister." I knew his sister was light skinned and very skinny, just like that girl. So we finally got out and into the restaurant and I needed to go to the restroom. Since I had on a romper, it was extra hard to go, not to mention the toilet was for the height of a one-year old and I had on heels. Thankfully, this experience was comical because it calmed my nerves. So I finally finished my business and washed my hands. Briana needed help putting in her contacts, but we eventually made our way out of the bathroom. We grabbed stools that were near the back of the bistro. He was already playing so we were enjoying the music and ordered buffalo chicken dip. We danced and sang along to the music and we were asked to take a picture with the rest of the ladies. So when we joined the other ladies, I got a better look at the girl that I thought was his sister. It wasn't his sister.

Of course, my mind went from 0 to 1,000 real quick. I start feeling stupid because I got all cute thinking I was coming to pull this man and he had a girlfriend. At least I presumed he did because she was following him around and was the first one at his side when he finished playing. That sounds like girlfriend stuff, right? Anyway, I had had enough and I told Briana I was ready to leave. We went outside and took a few pictures in the parking lot. I started to feel kind of tacky coming to his event and not speaking so before I pulled off, I got out of the car and as soon as I opened my mouth, the girl came out behind him. So with a cracked face, I pretended to look in my backseat for something. To avoid my whole face falling apart, I just got back in the driver's seat and drove off. The entire way home my mind was torn between listening to Briana's problems and deciding whether I should say anything to him. We finally made it back and I decided that I would at least tell him he did a great job. I sent him a message and he responded immediately. Over the course of three days, we had a short conversation and in my own slick way I found out that the girl was just a friend.

Although I was relieved about that, I still felt something strange because we weren't talking as much and he didn't ask for my number. I just knew he would have by now. He knew I was interested because a mutual friend of ours took it upon himself to relay that message to him. Since he didn't show any interest, I moved on. I wasn't going to chase him and I refused to make a fool of myself. By now you're probably wondering, "Why did she include this story if she didn't get the man?" Did I

LOVE FOR ALL THE WRONG REASONS

read your mind? This was God showing me, once again, that this is not my job. I figured going through the steps of understanding myself and gaining a better relationship with God had helped me obtain the ability to pick the right man. While I may have picked a good man, he was not *my* good man. Once again, I had to take a few steps back and wait. This experience reminded me that God always has the better plan.

The upshot is that in pursuit of the next relationship, don't limit yourself or the course of fate by thinking love only comes one way or that you have to conform to society's standards. Sometimes you have to step out of your comfort zone and take a leap of faith. For example, we hear and read Proverbs 18:22 (KJV) all the time and it is often misquoted. It says, "Whoso findeth a wife findeth a good thing, and obtaineth favour of the Lord." Usually we hear, "When a man findeth a wife..." to show that the man is the hunter and that he should be pursuing a woman.   While this may be biologically true, he still can't find you if you're hidden. He may not even notice you until you say something. I am not suggesting that you approach every guy you find attractive and ask him out on a date.   However, I am suggesting that you eliminate the stigma associated with it. Some men are shy in nature and it takes them a while to warm up to people and even gather the courage to say, "Hi." So I see no issue with making yourself noticeable. Once again, be available, but not desperate and be open to what God tells you in this process.

Don't be afraid to ask deep questions! Ask the guy what he refuses to compromise on, his biggest fear, something he wishes he had done differently. There is no need to dance around the idea of who he is; actually get to know him! Of course you're allowed to ask standard questions like where he is from, his favorite color, and his birthday, but those only scratch the surface of who he is. Just like you had to do a self-examination, you should feel comfortable enough to ask him the same questions you asked yourself. Being timid about it might alarm him more than you think. If you're only asking basic questions, how can he be sure that you want anything more than a temporary fix? The motive should not be to see how he measures up to your past relationships, but how he measures up to the needs of your future.

While you have to be careful not to compare your new companion to old ones, you still have to remember the lessons you've learned and how to avoid making the same mistakes. Remember that he or she is not the same person and allow them to gradually reveal themselves to you. At this point you are probably excited about starting something new, but you should not allow this to cloud your judgment. Everyone is who you want them to be at the beginning, so don't plan the wedding on Pinterest just yet. You shouldn't get so caught up in the future that you forget about the present. I'm not telling you to search out all their flaws because eventually they will become evident, but don't ignore the signs when they present themselves to you. Let actions speak louder than every word he or she speaks.

Let's say you meet this guy…he's handsome, has an established career, and a killer smile. He asks you out on a few dates and you oblige with no hesitation. Well, while you're out he decides that it's okay for him to flirt with other women or constantly give his cell phone more attention than he gives you. We could use the excuse that you two are not in a committed relationship, but who are we fooling? If he does these kinds of things now, what will he do if you both decide to become exclusive? Those two are not the only signs that you could see; it's up to you and your intuition to filter out what's worth your time. Sometimes we are aware of destructive situations long before we arrive at the stage of depression, anger, or hurt. All the same, we stay, thinking we can make the situation better or change our

---

LOVE FOR ALL THE WRONG REASONS

companions. We habitually make ourselves susceptible to any and every offensive thing that can be thrown at us.

When you look on social media and see comments under other females' or males' posts that offend you, how many times do you go back and look at it? As a matter of fact, have you deleted the screenshot? If a friend sends you a picture of your significant other out with someone else, how many times do you zoom in to make sure it's him or her? It's not going away and you're definitely not imagining it, but you can't stop looking at it. It's funny how we are always eager to see the very thing that will hurt us the most, but it is in this moment that we have to remember everything that we've gone through that got us to this point. Choosing to let his bad habits slide, allowing him to disregard our feelings, or changing our criteria so that it matches what he has to offer brought us here. Here is where it stops because this is where we have made the decision to understand ourselves, establish better standards, forgive those who hurt us, recognize that there are good men and women, and embrace the single life. We've gone through this process to be able to thoroughly enjoy the next relationship. Be mindful that you don't end up taking on a job because you want a boyfriend or a girlfriend. Being in a relationship should not turn you into a private

LOVE FOR ALL THE WRONG REASONS

investigator or a babysitter. This relationship should bring you joy and ease. If you are *searching* for discrepancies or any indication of him or her being the opposite of what they said, maybe you should rethink the whole thing. It's obvious that there still are some trust issues and insecurities there.

Do yourself and your new beau a favor and be free! Everything that you were afraid of should no longer bind you. The real, unfiltered, unapologetic you should be at the forefront, confident in who you are and what you need. The very thing that you are most embarrassed about should be one of the easiest things you can communicate with your new partner about. If he or she cannot handle you, be mature enough to let him or her go. You've taken enough time trying to figure yourself and your life out; you are not required to do the same for someone else. Your companion should bring out the best in you and help you substantially and sufficiently define what love is to you and for you. The most complex and unclear things should suddenly become embarrassingly simple. Get rid of all preconceptions and let the chips fall where they may. You'll see that happiness is now, and has always been, your own conscious decision.

LOVE FOR ALL THE WRONG REASONS

Sometimes People Do Change

Calm down, this chapter is not about to be a repeat of the last two years of my life. There were no second chances given to anyone who messed up the first time. However, *I* did get a second chance. Sometimes people actually do change and I had to remind myself of that when I reconnected with a young man I met in elementary school. Initially, I had no interest in him whatsoever. Throughout our years in school, I always thought he was too flirtatious with a side of promiscuity. He just wasn't my "type". I had predetermined that I needed a guy whose head was on straight (whatever that is in high school), who recognized the value of a real woman, and one who would not hurt me. Realistically, how often do you find that while you're in high school? I was way ahead of time! When we were in middle school, he transferred to another school before it was time for us to go to high school. Every chance he got, he made sure that I knew he was interested in me. I still wasn't paying attention because in my mind, he had played over and with too many females; I was not going to be added to that list.

LOVE FOR ALL THE WRONG REASONS

We graduated from high school and I would see him around every now and then, but being so deep in my own relationship and having the mindset that I had towards him, it didn't matter. He would even inbox me on Facebook every once in a while. Our interactions were far and few in between, and they returned to him fruitless, but he never gave up. When I shot him down one time, he'd be back a couple months later. I kept thinking, "When is this boy going to quit?" I went to college and so did he, but he soon joined the military. The only way I knew anything about what he was up to was by looking at his social media. Well, one day, I can't even remember when, his consistency worked. It caught me completely off guard, but after thinking about it I had to ask myself why I didn't give him a chance sooner. He was no longer the person I thought he was.

Because I participated in the process of understanding myself, I know what I am attracted to, and I realize the changes I have gone through. So now I had to give myself room to explore. I had a list of deal-breakers, but I had to remember to set reasonable standards because the truth is, you honestly don't know your perfect match until you've encountered them. Of course you have preferences, but you don't know what you can deal with until you're approached with it. When

I decided to be in another relationship I could hear myself saying, "He's not my type, but I don't want to be mean." I checked off my list of criteria and he didn't match up to what I had prematurely deemed as "important". Despite all that, I gave him a chance. As a result, I found that my values changed even more and my perspective of him changed with it. I was wrong about him, but being wrong never felt so good.

Over the course of approximately fifteen years, this boy, turned man, had changed my life in the most subtle and unexpected way. Through all those conversations of rejection, he somehow reached my heart and I couldn't deny that. My definition of love had already gone through an evolutionary phase, but with him it gained even more depth. He challenged me. Everything we brought to each other's attention posed questions that were relevant and conversations that stimulated our minds, bodies, and souls. It wasn't about who I thought I was, but he made me think about who I wanted to be and who I wanted to be with him. The most amazing thing to me was most of this occurred while he was all the way in Cuba! He had been deployed for one year, and during that time I only got to see him in person twice.

LOVE FOR ALL THE WRONG REASONS

Not only did I fall in love with him while he was a solid 800 miles away, I trusted him that far away as well. It may sound crazy to some, but it was one of the easiest things for me to do. The previous perspective that I held of him was only the subject in jovial matters. I never had to question his loyalty or wonder what he was doing or who he was with. My intuition never even gave any hints and it's usually spot on. I wondered if I had begun to shut my eyes to certain things due to this newfound fortune, but I couldn't find a legitimate reason or enough space for doubt. It was as if I had expected the very worst out of him because that's what I got from everyone else, but I was wrong. God had literally turned my misfortune into Fortune...no really, his last name is Fortune. Who would've thought?

We hear quite often that girls choose their husbands based on the father figure in their lives. For this reason, I have to thank my dad for being such a positive model in my life. I looked for a man that would work hard to provide, that would tell me the truth when I didn't want to hear it the most, and hoped that he was tall, dark, and handsome (two out three isn't too bad). I can confidently say that my Fortune has those traits. I have no question that he is willing to work hard to achieve his goals and he will tell me what I need to hear when I need

---

LOVE FOR ALL THE WRONG REASONS

to hear it. Because of my dad, I know what a real man is. Thank you, Daddy.   I can't thank my dad without thanking my mom. Never has there been a greater set of parents than the one I have. My mom is the epitome of the virtuous woman in Proverbs 31. There is nothing she can't do and I appreciate her for not hoarding the knowledge and wisdom that she has gained as a wife and mother. She has taught me how to conduct myself with grace and a hint of sass that is like no other personality you will ever encounter. Thank you, Mommy.

While the father figure is extremely important, it doesn't hurt to have a brother. My brother is the only guy that can aggravate me but make me love him even more while he does it. His opinion weighs a lot more than most people may think. Next to my dad, he is my protector and I appreciate him. I appreciate him for continuing the example that he saw in my dad. I am grateful to all three of them for exemplifying yet another form of love. They, too, have shown me how to forgive and see the best in people even after you've seen their worst. This, in part, is why I had faith in my Fortune and how I allowed my love to come full circle.

So here's the man I saw walking into my life bringing peace and love with him. From this point and for the rest of my natural life, I am confident in our love

LOVE FOR ALL THE WRONG REASONS

and its growth. Love does not always hit you in the face when it arrives. Sometimes it catches you off guard, but it always comes at the right time. I couldn't help but compare his pursuit of me to the way God pursued me. Time after time, I rejected God's love or seemed as if I wasn't ready. Each time He came back and showed me that I was still worthy of being loved. In this new relationship, I am confident in the very reasons we have learned to love each other and they are for the right reasons. I love him for his consistency, his mind, who he truly is, and not who I hope he will be, and his beard (just kidding, even though that adds a special touch). I love him for helping me see who I am and awakening a side of me that has been asleep for a long time. I love him because I can feel his love from 800 miles away. I love him because he trusts me and I can trust him. I love him because of his heart. Every word, and every deed has been genuine and it makes it hard not to love him back.

He loves me because of who he has become while he is with me. I remember him telling me, "I love you because here I saw a pure woman with a pure heart who had just healed from sever scarring. I felt that I had to give you what no one else did, what I never had…authenticity. You are my everything and I am literally nothing without you." There's nothing we won't do for each other, even if we fuss before we do it. There's nothing we won't debate, only to draw the conclusion that we both have valid points. There is no end to this love and I love the way forever is looking to me.

LOVE FOR ALL THE WRONG REASONS

Progress, Not Perfection

Although I was happy with my new relationship, I struggled. Throughout this entire book, I've encouraged you to trust the process, find yourself and what works for you. While all of that is vital to experiencing true love, you still have to take heed of the fact that it's still not going to be perfect. You have to let go of what you think a relationship should be and embrace what it really is for you, whatever it is. At the beginning, I told you what I thought love was; now I'm going to tell you what I thought a relationship was.

In order to call it a relationship I figured you had to know all of that person's favorites, their flaws, even know their family, and essentially you are able to answer a question about him or her in their absence. Wrong. You should know a lot of those things, but that is not the way you measure a relationship. I also used to think that posting your significant other on social media was one of the ways you were "supposed" to show that you love each other. Wrong again. Being with my Fortune was nothing like anything I had ever experienced. Our relationship defied every preconceived notion that I had about relationships.

LOVE FOR ALL THE WRONG REASONS

His demeanor as a man was completely different. While I knew he meant what he said and said what he meant, he had no problem apologizing when he was wrong. Honestly, he apologizes even when he's right. He took the time to figure out how I needed to be loved and every day he strives to be what I need. It's not about whether I know your favorite television show, or whether you decided to make me your "Woman Crush Wednesday"; it's about knowing your heart. Relationships are not defined by the rules of society, but by feelings and connections. We did not start off with this knowledge; we gained it. This is progress, not perfection.

Our relationship is far from perfect because every day we find something to debate or improve. However, that's a sign of people who want to be together and actually want to *stay* together. If you never tell your partner where you feel the relationship needs improvement, how will they know? If you've never told them how a certain comment has made you feel, how will they know? This is why you have to show them how to love you. He knew about the things I dealt with in the past and he knew how it damaged me. Since he knew all of this, he listened attentively to what was missing. He did not always get it right, but he always tried and that's what mattered to me. As I stated earlier, it is perfectly okay (and desirable) to teach someone how to love you. Your actions may not always come naturally because over time people change and so do their needs; you have to adapt to their love language if you're willing to continue loving them.

We cannot forget about the importance of communication. At first, I thought he was the most difficult person I had ever met, and he thought I was the meanest person he had ever encountered. Even though these opinions haven't changed, we've learned how to communicate with each other so that it doesn't turn into a screaming match. Through many conversations we've learned each other's boundaries and we choose not to hit below the belt. We have every right to get upset about certain things, but we have both agreed that before we stop talking, the problem has to be solved. This means no one is walking away and no one is handing out the silent treatment. Refusing to work through a problem can lead you down many roads, but reconciliation is not one of them.

His deployment could possibly be one of the best things that has ever happened to us. Don't get me wrong, it is extremely hard to love on him 800 miles away, but that's the best challenge. If I can show him I love him that far away, who could imagine what it will be like when he gets home? Too often we take for granted the opportunity we have to show people we care for them when they are right in front of us. When we lose them, we start to think of all that we could've, should've, and would've done if we had known that we'd lose them sooner rather than later. Each day we show each other how we feel by working towards our future together and respecting one another in our conversations. We both know what our lives were like before we came together, which only makes our desire to stay together even stronger.

Do away with the box that you've put relationships in! Stop relying on romantic movies to tell you what love is and what it should look like. To be forthright, don't rely on this book either. I've given you a description of what it is for me; that does not mean that it's going to be the same for you. Stop relying on Facebook, or *any* social media outlet for that matter, to let you know what's real. Sure, posting your relationship can be cute, but that does not make it exempt from issues. We have to learn to draw the line between posting because we want to and posting to prove something to people. Newsflash: a lot of people honestly don't care

LOVE FOR ALL THE WRONG REASONS

about your relationship. If they do, it's often only to see when something goes wrong.

Starting over with someone else means getting used to them and learning about him or her. Make sure you're doing this with someone who is worth your time. The usual in relationships for me was starting off getting those sweet messages when I woke up, then it would die down. Guys would be the sweetest at the beginning and end up being disturbingly anal at some point. As a result of this routine, I waited. I waited before I fell in love and carefully observed him. I needed to see that his actions matched with his words. I did not *expect* him to become that guy, but I wanted to be prepared if he did. Thankfully, he hasn't become that guy.

Even though my words make me sound like I had become an expert at getting over the hurt and moving on, it still took me a while to put it all into action. Once again, I was making progress, not perfection. Going through the processes I have described does not automatically put you in the position to love like you've never been hurt. Unless a tragedy occurs that causes you to forget, you will always remember what you went through even after forgiveness has been completed. It is your truth, not your tragedy.

LOVE FOR ALL THE WRONG REASONS

What I've Learned

Twenty-two years of figuring myself out, five years of lessons learned, and God knows how many more years to go. It was all worth it. It *is* all worth it. Of course I couldn't see that while I was going through it, but it has all worked out for my good just like God promised. This process has taught me so much about God and myself. I know who he is and I know who I am. I have to thank him because I can't think of a better way to get to know him than to need him. Yes, someone else's story could be worse than mine; but I had to do this for myself and the benefit of others who may be experiencing a similar heartbreak. Each story is different, but we all learn a similar lesson.

Relationships can be beautiful and rewarding. They can make you face things about yourself that you want to ignore. Last, but definitely not least, they can teach you unforgettable lessons. Trust your instincts, they're often quite right. Be reminded that the vibes you pick up on are not mistakes, so protect your spirit and your heart. Proverbs 4:23 says, "Keep thy heart with all diligence; for out of it are the issues of life." Every person that you associate yourself with has a purpose in your life, whether it takes one day or a few years to fulfill their purpose, they have one. My ex fulfilled his purpose by showing me that even after pain, there is a reward that is worth getting through the process for. He showed me that your first love is not always your last. Through the many obstacles we faced as a couple, it has become more and more clear to me that a man will change for the woman he really wants. If it were in my power, I am not sure that going through all of this would be my first choice in learning this lesson. However, I would not take any of it back, especially because of the place and the person it brought me to.

My family and friends taught me how to forgive and love one another in spite of all our flaws, differences, and mistakes. Forgiveness is one of the toughest powers to master, but it is also one of the most essential. It has made me stronger and it has helped me maintain self-control. Whenever someone has mistreated me, I can easily forgive them and not allow their presence to change my mood. My Fortune taught me that love doesn't take on real, indescribable meaning until you find the right one to love. Love for you can only be defined by you, and of course I have my own definition and imagination of what it is, but he became love personified for me. Whatever love can be, he is. When I get ahead of myself or lose track of what is really important, he always brings it back to my attention. I remember asking questions about when he thinks certain things should happen and he finally told me to focus on the love, not the timeline. It was so simple, but it meant so much. I couldn't argue with that, especially after saying it myself earlier in this book: "You shouldn't get so caught up in the future that you forget about the present."

Finally, God has shown and continues to show me his incomparable power. Sometimes that's all it really is. We question, "Why me?" It's not always *because* it's you, it could be because it's *Him*. In the midst of all this, I had to be reminded that He is God and He has all power. His lesson for me was to trust Him even when I don't understand. In the back of my mind, I knew everything would be fine, but I didn't know when. I believe that's what bothered me the most. It seemed as if time had slowed down and He had turned a deaf ear to my prayer. All the while He listened to every detail and put them all in corporeal form with my Fortune. He applied pressure to iron out the wrinkles in my life and to give me an inspirational testimony. Now I am able to encourage others who may be experiencing a storm and tell them that it doesn't last forever. On the other side of it, you find peace of mind and a clear conscience. No one could teach this lesson better than God.

LOVE FOR ALL THE WRONG REASONS

Everything eventually works out. It may not happen when you want it to, but it always happens at the right time. I was filled with animosity and approaching a place of isolation, but that is when everything changed. When you want to give up, always find a reason to hold on just a little while longer. As Dr. Maya Angelou said, "Have enough courage to trust love one more time and always one more time." Discover who you are, what you love, how you love, and what you need. Heal thoroughly, forgive wholeheartedly, and be free. You are not a victim and try your best not to be a vilifier. Trust God, trust yourself, and trust the process. You don't figure love out, you *feel* it out. In the end, make sure you love right, and love strong.

LOVE FOR ALL THE WRONG REASONS

About The Author

Alethia C. Smith is a native of Bishopville, SC. After receiving her bachelor's degree in Psychology from Wingate University, she returned home and began work as a secretary. She experienced what she believes was a great deal of hurt and found a way to turn this negative event into a positive one by writing this book. Experiencing that same hurt allowed her to find her passion and purpose in life: helping other people and altering perspectives. Her faith in God and herself brought her to a place of peace and she chose to share it with others in this book and on her blog, *Charnell's Choices*. She hopes to continue writing and inspiring others through her transparency and willingness to be used by God.

www.ingramcontent.com/pod-product-compliance
Lightning Source LLC
Chambersburg PA
CBHW051833040426
42447CB00006B/514